To Bonnie —
Best Wishes
Betty C. Hearnes

Warren Eastman Hearnes

A Memoir

by **Rob Crouse**
from the Personal Notes and Recollections of
Betty C. Hearnes

Best Regards
Warren E. Hearnes

DEDICATION TO BETTY COOPER HEARNES

❝ There are lists to dedicate this book to, but only one woman ultimately saw that it got finished. I am dedicating the book to her.

She always believed in me and kept my feet on the ground. We have lived about 60 years together after only three dates – that's pretty good in today's world, but whether we get one more year or thirty years, it has been a ride of a lifetime.

I did my part and Betty did hers and most everyone else's. ❞

To BCH from Well

Thanks for the memories.

WARREN EASTMAN HEARNES

ISBN 978-1-60461-393-3

BOOK and JACKET DESIGN, COMPOSITION and PRODUCTION DIRECTION by 94 DESIGN • MARTHASVILLE • MISSOURI

TYPE SET in OPTIMA

FIRST EDITION (1M) 2007 and SECOND EDITION (1M) 2007 PRINTED and BOUND by WALSWORTH PUBLISHING • MARCELINE • MISSOURI

Contents

Prologue

9   Chapter One: Beginnings

19   Chapter Two: Preparation

33   Chapter Three: Coordination, Conflict & Collaboration

45   Chapter Four: A New Era–A New Style of Leadership

61   Chapter Five: Out of the Shadows

73   Chapter Six: A "Real Education Governor"

84   Pictorial Section

119   Chapter Seven: Programs and Progress

137   Chapter Eight: Partners In Public Service and In Life

157   Chapter Nine: Readjustments

165   Chapter Ten: Legacy

171   *Afterword*

175   *Acknowledgements*

Prologue
by Senator Tom Eagleton

I remember the first time I met Warren E. Hearnes. It was in 1957, half a century ago, when I was the young Circuit Attorney of St. Louis. I was in Jefferson City, lobbying for a bill in the state legislature, the substance of which I cannot now remember. I was seated in the office of State Representative Tom "Kind Words" Walsh. I gave Walsh that nickname because he was often denouncing some politician, or some bill in the legislature, or something else. In walked Warren. At that time, he was the Democratic Majority Leader of the Missouri House of Representatives. We had heard of each other. Walsh blurted out, "Okay, Mr. Big City Boy, meet Mr. Country Boy." We shook hands. And that is how a 50-year friendship began.

We both were ambitious. We both had politics in our blood. We both wanted to move ahead, following parallel paths that we hoped would lead to success.

Our goals were divergent. I was interested in national issues and hoping to eventually get to the United States Senate. Warren was interested in state issues and his goal was to be Governor. We were not contesting rivals, but we did keep an eye on each other, as the nature of politics requires politicians to do.

What I saw, when I kept my eye on Warren, was that he was the master of the Missouri House of Representatives. He knew the rules, the traditions, the angles, and the pitfalls of the profession of legislation. Yes, legislation is a profession. Just as medicine is divided into numerous specialties, the process of legislating is a professional specialty of politicians. You have to know when to submit the right bill at the right place and the right time. A successful legislative leader knows how to do this based on his experience and instincts. Warren had an innate sense of what would sell and what wouldn't.

Warren wanted to be a two-term governor, two consecutive terms. Missouri tradition was one term and out. Governor Phil Donnelly was elected twice, but Governor Forrest Smith served a term in between Donnelly's terms. The principal impediment to Warren's goal of abolishing the single-term tradition was Senator Mike Kinney of St. Louis. Kinney ultimately served 55 consecutive years in the Missouri Senate, a world record. He was, on the state level, Missouri's "wise man," just as Missouri's Clark Clifford was the "wise man" of Truman-era Washington.

Warren romanced old Kinney with just the right touch–not too sweet, not too overt, just right. Kinney was Missouri's living history and, unless he could be persuaded, Warren's two consecutive term proposal was dead on arrival.

I was his Lieutenant Governor and I watched the Hearnes legislative program move smoothly through the legislature at the behest of a Governor who had the enhanced clout that came with the prospect of a re-election bid at the end of his first term.

On the final night of the 1965 legislative session, the Senate passed the 19th of Warren's 20 major proposals. It took some arm-twisting, but Warren got it done.

Missouri had never seen anything like it. People around Jefferson City talked of the "Hearnes Touch," that instinctive quality of judgment that separates a great practitioner of legislation from the good practitioner.

The only comparison I can make to Warren is Lyndon Johnson at the height of his legislative career. Read Robert A. Caro's book, *Master of the Senate: The Years of Lyndon Johnson*. There you will see the "Johnson Touch" and can better understand its Missouri counterpart.

In 1968, both the governorship and a seat in the U.S. Senate were up for election. Ed Long, the incumbent U.S. Senator, had created some personal problems for himself. Warren could have easily defeated Long if he were to seek the Senate seat.

We sat on an old wooden swing outside the Governor's mansion. There was a third person with us, Gene Walsh, Hearnes' counselor and a mutual friend. We talked politics. I wanted to run in the Democratic primary against Ed Long, but I wanted to be absolutely certain that Warren wasn't going to do so. I was not going to take him on, as popular as he was.

Warren made it clear that his goal was to be Missouri's first two-term governor (in succession). He went on to give me some sound advice, "Tom, you're not going to get a seat in the Senate on a silver platter. You have to fight for it. You have to take a chance if you think the timing is right. You have to sense it in your gut."

Warren is not a bragger. That's his nature. He's more Paul Newman than Lee Iacocca. Take it from me, as one who has loved politics as much as Warren, you are about to read about the most intuitive, most creative, and most accomplished governor in 20th century Missouri history.

Thomas F. Eagleton

Tom Eagleton died in March 2007.

Prologue photo – Missouri's U.S. Senator Tom Eagleton
on the Senate floor, 1986. • From the Hearnes Personal Collection

CHAPTER ONE
Beginnings

WARREN EASTM

CHARLESTON, MISSOURI

From high school to the Un
Army to West Point is a sy
date. He found that social life
lacking and academics sadly pr
he was determined to make goo
he did, and he still found time
week-ends. His love of mili
ness, his high sense of d
all problems that conf

success

*"You don't work for yourself.
You work for your family.
I wanted my family to be proud of me.
That's my satisfaction."*

WARREN HEARNES

Montage of photos on previous page –

From bottom – The HEARNES FAMILY
Left to right – Bob, Richard, Mr. and Mrs. E. B. Hearnes, Donald,
Eleanor Hearnes Hequembourg, and Warren, circa 1950;

West Point yearbook;

Graduation from U.S Military Academy at West Point; and

As a freshman at Charleston High School, 1938.

From the Hearnes Personal Collection

A ll people have defining moments in their lives. Some of those moments are by design—a goal, a plan, or a realization. Some of those moments come through circumstances—the influence of another person, an event, or merely the times in which we live. The life of Warren Eastman Hearnes was shaped by both.

Warren was born on July 24, 1923 to Earle and Edna Hearnes of Charleston, Missouri. However, the birth took place in Moline, Illinois. Edna had chosen to return to the hospital of her hometown to give birth to her fifth child.

Upon Warren's birth, his father sent a telegram back home to inform the family that read: "Just had a boy—will trade same for bulldog."

> *Just had a boy– will trade same for bulldog.*
>
> *EARLE HEARNES*

As this sense of humor would indicate, Earle Hearnes was an affable person...well liked in the community. Because of his small stature, most people in the area called him "Shorty."

Edna Hearnes was well known for her work ethic. She had a reputation of being one of the hardest working women in Mississippi County, and she tried to instill that quality in Warren. At one point in Warren's young life, Edna thought it would be a good idea for him to join her in the little business endeavor of raising chickens. However, Warren, politically astute even at an early age, appeared to get the best out of the partnership. Edna fed the chickens, cleaned the hen house, and put her hands under the hens to collect the eggs, while Warren assumed the more glamorous and profitable end of the business. He sold the eggs and collected the money.

When Warren was very young, his father owned two stores—one in Charleston and one in East Prairie. Both Earle and Edna worked at the stores to make them successful. Fortunately for the couple, Earle's mother, known to everyone as "Teeny," came to live with the family after the death of her husband, and she assumed the primary responsibility of rearing the Hearnes brood—particularly the two youngest, Warren and his brother Bob. "Teeny" would live with the family, helping with the household, until her death.

Warren proudly gave himself the nickname of "Scarface" at an early age, the result of an accident at the age of three. He was running with a quart jar and fell on it, creating a long scar on his right cheek that even a large number of stitches could not erase.

The HUNTER STREET GANG • circa 1930
From the Hearnes Personal Collection

Warren and Bob grew up savoring all the joys that small town rural life affords young men. They played baseball and basketball, fished, and swam with the other neighborhood boys. These boyhood friends were better known as "The Hunter Street Gang," because they were constantly seeking each other's company and all lived on or near Hunter Street. (The Hearnes family lived on nearby Byrd Avenue.)

One of the most vivid memories of that time for Warren was belonging to a group comparable to today's scout troops called the "Indian Guides." Each of the boys and their fathers were given a Native American name. Warren was known as "White Eagle," brother Bob went by "Swift Eagle," and Earle Hearnes, known for his scarcity of hair, was called the very descriptive "Bald Eagle."

Earle's one major hobby was playing golf—a passion Warren would inherit. The only difference was Warren played right-handed, and his father was a "lefty."

Life was comfortable for the Hearnes family until national events forced the family to, as Warren so tactfully expressed it, "live a different way." The coming of The Great Depression dramatically changed the life of the Hearnes family, like most American families of the time. Earle Hearnes lost both his stores, and the family lost their home. Earle took a job with the Bertrand Cotton Company, and Edna, ever the businesswoman, sold cakes, pies, and potato chips to local stores. Seeing how his parents fought back to overcome these difficult times would have a profound effect on young Warren, sparking his desire to be successful.

During Warren's adolescence, another event in his parents' life would have a great influence as well. His father Earle ran for and won the position of County Clerk of Mississippi County and served several terms. His father's joy in campaigning and public service were not lost on Warren.

> **"Bob and I didn't take as much time with our lessons as we should have."**
>
> WARREN HEARNES

One of the most important memories Warren has of his grandmother "Teeny" was her preoccupation with school grades. She talked about the importance of good grades constantly, and when school report cards were handed out, getting by "Teeny" without a detailed inspection and discussion of classes and grades was a mission impossible. Fortunately, for both Warren and Bob, their grades in elementary school were satisfactory. Later on, in high school, that status would change.

As Warren politely put it, "Bob and I didn't take as much time with our lessons as we should have." He would regret that lapse later in life when he struggled academically at West Point.

Attending West Point, or at least pursuing a military career, was a dream of Warren's after he sat through a movie about the academy as a boy. When talk came of mobilizing the National Guard for the wartime efforts, Warren enlisted even though, at 16, he was not old enough to serve. The local company commander, a family friend, had overlooked the age requirement, but the discovery was made when Warren's guard unit was called to action and sent to Camp Robinson in Little Rock, Arkansas. The disappointed seventeen year old was sent home just in time for high school graduation with a discharge for minority reasons.

After high school graduation, Warren enrolled at the University of Missouri where he attended school for a year and a half until he was drafted. He reported for duty and was sent to Fort Sheridan, Illinois.

Ironically, just as he was finally in the military, his life took a defining turn. He received a telegram from U.S. Congressman Orville Zimmerman that President Roosevelt had appointed him to West Point. His childhood dream had been realized.

Later, the glory of the moment would be somewhat diminished when Warren found out he was actually third on the list for the appointment. The other two candidates ahead of him had been disqualified. Fate had played a decisive role in the future of Warren Hearnes.

Warren reported to West Point in 1943. While academics were often a struggle, he did succeed. Perhaps the best outcome for Warren at West Point was the power of reasoning he acquired there. Warren said, "I developed the power of analysis so the mind can reason to a logical conclusion. Then once the conclusion was reached, I never wavered."

This ability would hold him in good stead throughout his public life. Whenever a decision was to be made, Warren Hearnes would gather all the facts, listen to all sides, and then take decisive action, never wavering until the business was concluded.

Warren likes to tell the story of having a little fun at the expense of one West Point plebe when he was an upper class cadet. Knowing the young man two years behind Warren was from his hometown, Warren came up behind the young man, changed his voice, and commanded him to "halt." Once the young plebe snapped to attention, Warren asked him where he was from.

WARREN HEARNES – Graduation from U.S. Military Academy at West Point
From the Hearnes Personal Collection

When the young man answered "Charleston," Warren said, "Never heard of it," and walked away.

After earning his B.S. degree at West Point in 1946, Warren graduated as an infantry officer and was sent by the U.S. Army for his first tour of duty with the 35th Division to Puerto Rico. Although he would advance to the rank of First Lieutenant, Warren would suffer a freak accident in 1947 that would send him in the direction he was destined to take—a fulfilling professional life in politics and a fulfilling personal life with his wife Betty.

The event occurred during a friendly game of softball with his men in Puerto Rico. A first sergeant was chasing a fly ball and ran right into Warren. "I was at second base and collided with the right fielder and broke my right ankle," Warren recalls.

The Army doctors who treated Warren did a mediocre job at best, and the resulting complications forced an eventual military flight to Battle Creek, Michigan, where Warren spent months enduring a bone graft and a slow healing broken bone. He was sent home to Charleston to recuperate at the end of 1947, but the injury would be a source of problems his entire life, leaving him with a slight limp.

❝I knew who he was, of course. Didn't like him very much either.❞

BETTY HEARNES

While he was convalescing, Warren noticed a young woman in his hometown named Betty Cooper, daughter of the Charleston Baptist minister, Rev. A. B. Cooper. A vivacious brunette with freckles, Betty was home on spring break from Baylor University where she was pursuing a music degree.

Betty's family had moved to Charleston when she was five and Warren was nine, and as in most small towns, the Hearnes and Cooper families certainly knew each other. "The night I graduated from grade school, Warren graduated from high school," Betty remarks. "I knew who he was, of course. Didn't like him very much either."

Obviously, the families had no connections. The Hearnes were Methodists, the Coopers Baptists. More significantly, the Hearnes were staunch Democrats and the Coopers rock-ribbed Republicans.

"This was in Charleston, Missouri, where you could hardly find any Republican," Betty explains. "Warren used to say: 'How in the world did

I ever find a Republican to marry in Mississippi County?' In 1952, my father was Republican chairman for the county and my brother-in-law was Democratic chairman. You should have the family to dinner under those circumstances."

Nevertheless, Warren Hearnes would be responsible for not just changing Betty Cooper's politics, but her mind where he was concerned. That spring vacation, Lieutenant Hearnes asked Betty for a date, and she turned him down. "I initially thought he was conceited," Betty says. "But I think that was because he's soft spoken and a little shy right at first."

In May, Betty returned home from college for summer vacation and ran into Warren on Main Street. Again, he asked her out. "I couldn't very well say no because he knew I had just gotten home from school," Betty admits. The date occurred, and by the third date, Warren had proposed. "I did say I'd have to think about it," Betty remembers. "So I thought about it for two nights." Then she accepted.

The couple actually dated for only three weeks because Warren was back at the hospital in Battle Creek for one week of the month. Nevertheless, with him scheduled to return to Puerto Rico for active duty, the wedding was set for July 2, much to Betty's parents' dismay.

Betty describes her parents' reaction as: "Waaaaaak! They nearly fainted. They liked him. But needless to say, they thought it was a little quick."

The wedding took place in one of the 14 churches that Rev. Cooper helped build—New Bethel Baptist Church. Rev. Cooper officiated. In fact, the ceremony was quite a family affair. Betty's sister was the maid of honor. One of her brothers gave her away. Two other sisters were in charge of the music. "That way you don't have to pay musicians," Betty explained.

Following the service, as Betty remembers it, she went to Puerto Rico, and her mother went to bed, brought prone by the anxiety that her daughter had rushed into a relationship that might not last. Betty's father simply called her by her nickname and said: "Peach, that will be a lesson to you."

Evidently, it proved to be a good lesson as Warren and Betty became lifelong partners. Many would say they were meant to be together. The signs are there. They even share the same birthday.

Concessions were made as well. The fall of 1948, Betty Hearnes, a 20-year-old Republican who had never voted in her life, cast her first official ballot for the Democratic Party. Warren Hearnes, who even taught Sunday school in the Methodist Church, joined the Baptist Church.

Betty soon settled into being an Army wife, and the Hearnes were blessed with their first daughter Lynn, while Warren was stationed in Puerto Rico. Unfortunately, Warren's leg never healed, and he was given a medical discharge in 1949. His dream of a military career had been dashed at the age of 27.

After returning to Missouri in January, 1950, Warren and Betty decided the next step was to finish their educations. They moved to Columbia so Warren could pursue his law degree at the University of Missouri and Betty could finish her music degree. But they soon found that going to school at that point in their lives was quite different. "When you have a family—wife, child, and another one on the way (Leigh, born in 1952)—it's not like going to MU single," Warren chuckles.

> **" I want to be governor of this state. "**
>
> *WARREN HEARNES*
> *AGE 29*

The couple had to find a way to support their family. As they discussed their options, their mutual interest in politics and the proximity of the State Capitol in Jefferson City brought the solution into view. Warren would run for the state legislature. So Warren filed his candidacy to represent his beloved Bootheel in the Missouri House of Representatives. He won that race and prepared to enter the House chambers as the youngest person ever to represent Mississippi County in the state legislature.

Yet with that win, Warren revealed another decision he had made, but only to Betty and a few close friends. No one else would know about that decision for another ten years.

"I want to be governor of this state," Warren told them. "And from now on, I'm going to work in that direction."

The seeds of destiny for Warren Eastman Hearnes were sown.

CHAPTER TWO
Preparation

"Make sure the fight is worth winning."
WARREN HEARNES

A fter taking the oath of office in January, 1951, the 27-year-old "Gentleman from Mississippi" came to the floor of the Missouri House of Representatives full of energy and ready to take on anyone. In his first term, Warren was afflicted with what veteran legislators call "microphonitus." As Warren remembers it, "I thought people wanted to hear all I had to say on an issue. After my first term, I learned other legislators really didn't care to hear all I had to say."

Yet that first term, his fellow House members soon learned Warren was ready to use the mike to comment on every issue that came to the floor and not shy about telling legislative veterans how operations could be improved. This brashness endeared him to no one, except perhaps *The Kansas City Star*, which named him "Outstanding Freshman Legislator."

"I talked more as a first term freshman than I did as House Majority Floor Leader my last year," Warren laughed.

Certainly, there had to be days when the young legislator, who was also juggling family responsibilities and law school, was operating on pure adrenaline. "Lots of nights after committee hearings, he'd drive back to Columbia at 1 a.m., study until 5, go to class, and then leave at noon to go back to Jefferson City," Betty recalls. "I don't know how he got through, but he did."

In those days, legislative sessions were not limited to five and one-half months as today. In Warren's first term, the legislature was in session eighteen months.

Fortunately, that grueling cycle ended with the close of his first term and graduation from law school in 1952. However, Warren still had to find a way to supplement his $125 a month legislator's salary so he opened a law practice in East Prairie, which would last for the next eight years of his legislative tenure. Every weekend, he would make the 300-mile trek from Jefferson City to his law practice to make ends meet. Betty, who had also finished her degree, taught vocal music in Charleston and later in Sikeston. The couple also built a home in Charleston.

Warren's ten years in the state legislature were marked by great achievement. He successfully fought to establish the University Medical School in Columbia and was a champion of mental health improvements. He sponsored a majority of the bills to improve public school education, including the Missouri Teachers' Retirement System—still considered one of the best in the country. He also was the principal sponsor of Amendment 4, which allowed municipalities to issue their own bonds for industrial development.

By the time his decade with the legislature had ended, Hearnes had introduced 52 bills, co-authored 114 bills, and guided 241 bills through the General Assembly. Twenty-two pieces of Hearnes legislation had been signed into law.

❝ I decided to become the best legislator in the rear ranks Missouri ever had. ❞

WARREN HEARNES

With his third term, Warren was chomping at the bit for more responsibility. He sought the Majority Floor Leader position, but was rebuffed. In 1955, he was defeated in the race to be floor leader. "That was a heartbreak," Warren reflects. "I was too young and got only a handful of votes. I didn't want to go through such heartbreak again." So for the first time in his life, Warren Hearnes took a step back.

"I began to look at myself and the role I could play," Hearnes said. "I decided to become the best legislator in the rear ranks Missouri ever had."

As a result, his colleagues eventually asked him to become Majority Floor Leader, rather than his vying for the opportunity. He became the first person ever to be elected Majority Floor Leader twice with no opposition.

His last two legislative terms, in 1957 and 1959, he became a master of parliamentary procedure and legislative negotiations. Once when Hearnes was Floor Leader and Richard Ichord was Speaker, they found themselves on opposite sides of a bill. The debate became intense, and they finally had to recess the House to call Congressman Clarence Cannon, Parliamentarian of the U.S. House of Representatives, to receive a determination on parliamentary procedure for this particular trucking bill. Warren was the sponsor of the bill and quite relieved when Cannon came down on his side in ruling on the point of order.

Another time, once again on a trucking bill, Warren called for the bill only to find it had disappeared. Upon examination, it was found the House Chief Clerk had left the chamber with the bill. Warren sent the Sergeant-At-Arms to find the Clerk and the bill. When the investigator returned, he reported to Warren that the bill had been taken to the Senate. But once Warren sent word to the Senate for its return, word came back that this august body knew nothing about either the whereabouts of the bill or the House Clerk. Finally, the mystery was solved when it was discovered the Clerk and the missing measure were cooling their heels in a *different* Senate—a downtown cocktail lounge bearing the same name.

Warren gradually became known as an expert on the rules and very efficient at running the House floor business. One colleague said Warren was the best Floor Leader he had ever seen. He observed that if a representative ever got in trouble during debate on a bill that he or she was sponsoring, Hearnes would take over the debate, work on the bill, and turn the proposal back to its sponsor with the sponsor still unaware of what had transpired. The *St. Louis Globe Democrat* recognized Hearnes as the most effective House member in debate and with good reason.

The most important result of Warren's ten years in the House was the excellent preparation it gave him for what lay ahead. He understood the legislature and its inner workings so when he became Governor, he knew what had to occur to get his legislative agenda through the process.

Of equal significance, he made great friends—friends on both sides of the aisle and in every county. His reputation for fairness, honesty, and keeping his word were universally known. On issues where party lines did not need to be drawn, Warren would often reach out to help a Republican. He also developed relationships with many of the Senators in the sister legislative body. Ultimately, all these friends would help him in his run for Governor and work with him on gubernatorial achievements, once he reached the Chief Executive office.

The other major gift that came out of those legislative years for the Hearnes was their third daughter, Julie B., born in 1958.

When the tumultuous Sixties came on the horizon, Warren was restless as well. He recognized that if he was to realize his aspiration to become Governor, the next step had to be taken. He had to gain statewide recognition and have statewide campaign experience. Once again, fate stepped in.

Walter Toberman had held the office of Secretary of State for many years. Serious health problems prompted him to announce he would not run again in 1960.

Seeing an opening with no statewide incumbent as a barrier, Warren jumped into the race. In the primary, he only carried 18 of the state's 114 counties but he showed great strength in the City of St. Louis where he had the powerful support of St. Louis political giants John (Doc) Lawler, Representative Thomas Walsh, and Midge Berra. Warren Hearnes was the Democratic winner over news editor James Kirkpatrick of Windsor, and in November, he easily won his first statewide election. Kirkpatrick had many friends in the newspaper business. Hearnes counted about 395 newspapers against him and a handful, five, in his corner. But he had his friends from law school, the legislature, the powerful St. Louis supporters, and $12,000 to spend. In those days, a race could be won with hard work and good friends.

Behind the scenes, Warren had already taken the preliminary steps for a gubernatorial run in 1964 before his general election win as Secretary of State. At that time, winning the Democratic primary for a statewide office meant the candidate could start measuring the office for drapes. With weak Republican support statewide, the general election was just the final affirmation.

So Warren began to meet with those key leaders from St. Louis as well as some outstate to build a team of supporters. "The Secretary of State was a tremendous experience," Hearnes relates. "I learned that nobody ever heard of the Majority Leader. It was the urban areas and my friends in St. Louis that carried me. The big realization was that I wasn't known in rural Missouri."

As Secretary of State, Warren set out to remedy that problem. For his first two years in office, practically every night he would leave the office after work for some outstate event where he could deliver his message and meet people.

Then, in 1962, two years before the next general election, Warren announced he was running for Governor. This time, however, the announcement to seek the highest office in the state was not met with blessings and good wishes. It hit like a bombshell. The road to victory was difficult and fraught with peril. This was not the way Democratic politics were played in the state of Missouri. For over twenty years, the person selected to be the Democratic nominee had been handpicked by an exclusive coalition of powerful bankers, attorneys, and politicians known as The Establishment. They controlled the party money and machinery. This selection process had always worked successfully, avoiding acrimonious party divisions and primary battles and keeping an orderly line of succession in place. Now Warren Hearnes was bucking the system. The candidate blessed by The Establishment was Lt. Governor Hilary Bush, a Kansas City lawyer groomed for the job and placed in the line of succession after Lieutenant Governor Edward V. Long went to the U.S. Senate.

Undaunted, Warren forged ahead in spite of a raft of warnings and protests. When people would say Bush looked, spoke, and acted like a Governor, Warren would ask: "But does he think like a Governor?"

The official announcement of his campaign was held at the Sikeston Armory with Missouri baseball legends Stan Musial and Joe Garagiola at his side.

The days were long and often discouraging as Warren and Betty barnstormed the state, scouring for votes. Sometimes they traveled in a small twin-engine plane. But most of the time, they appeared in their Mercury without air conditioning and a red, white, and blue campaign logo painted on the side.

Hearnes campaign strategy was genius. With so many organized Democrats failing to get behind him, he started Hearnes for Governor clubs in almost every county, recruiting many people to the campaign who had never worked in politics before. These committees worked tirelessly with the Hearnes to organize events, raise money for newspaper and radio ads, answer telephones and make calls, and get the voters out on election day. The committees had Warren's attention and their loyalty and energy seemed unlimited.

Hearnes recognized the importance of St. Louis from his successful race for secretary of state. So with the northeast, northwest, central and southeast parts of the state humming along with committee activity, Hearnes worked the city wards of St. Louis himself. If he got the endorsement of a ward's committeemen, that was great. If not, he organized a "rump" group to work the ward for him. Because the rumps were outsiders, they were freshly motivated and felt the challenge of bringing in a victory for their candidate, Warren Hearnes.

Another key in the election was St. Louis County. A group of twelve young men made it their mission to win the county. Theirs was a masterful piece of work, attending township meetings, raising money, and representing Hearnes whenever he couldn't be there himself. They shared his passion and his dream and communicated it wherever they went.

There were campaign rallies all over the state, sometimes with as many as two thousand enthusiastic supporters. This surprised the established political organizations, used to pulling these strings.

The difference in the candidates' campaigns soon became apparent. Here were Warren and Betty, arriving in a car with no air conditioning to shake hands with workers at factories, mills, and railroad yards and visit schools. In comparison, Hilary Bush would pull up in an air-conditioned sedan to hobnob with the elite Democratic contributors. This contrast was not lost on Warren, who fired up his rhetoric. "Are we going to have puppet government or people government?" he roared at every stop. "We in Missouri have an election...not a selection."

> ❝ *We in Missouri have an election, not a selection.* ❞
>
> WARREN HEARNES

His platform was comprehensive and appealing. Warren stood for four year colleges in Joplin and St. Joseph, development of the Meramec River Basin, levees and an access road for the Columbia Bottoms in St. Louis, lower tuition fees at state colleges, an improved prison and parole system, a stronger Human Rights Commission, more funds for public schools, a Missouri River bridge at St. Joseph, a program for those with mental disabilities, and pay increases for state hospital workers. Most important of all, he made a "no tax increase" pledge.

Nevertheless, many days Warren wondered if his message was resonating out there, reaching the voters he desperately needed to hear him. One evening, when the couple had a few quiet hours to themselves in a Kansas City hotel room, Warren turned to Betty in despair and exclaimed, "Betty, how am I going to get my name in the paper so people will know I'm a candidate?"

Betty, always the one with a quip to lighten the mood when needed, replied, "Well, maybe you could push me out the window."

Warren considered for a minute and then responded, "No. That won't do. They would print 'An unidentified woman fell out a window.'"

One of the advantages Warren did have was the ability to criticize the way government was operating. Bush, totally tied to the current Governor Dalton, who was supporting him, had to remain silent. This was particularly helpful to Warren when the candidates debated.

Another advantage was being the underdog and the rebel. He was "the outsider," bucking the establishment. He was the populist candidate...the man of the people ready to fight for their concerns against the wealthy special interests. This appealed to a large segment of the Democratic Party.

However, Warren's secret weapon was definitely Betty, who delighted the crowd with her plain speaking and good humor. One weekend, Betty drove 1,000 miles, traveling across the state. She attended 14 coffees in St. Louis in one day. "Usually, I'm in charge of bringing the supplies," Betty shared with a reporter. "I told Warren all I wanted for Christmas was a nice, lightweight, aluminum stepladder so I could put up posters. That big staff you read that candidates have—well, we were it."

The opposition grumbled: "We'd give her an all expense paid trip to Europe if we could get rid of her until the election is over."

> " *I told Warren all I wanted for Christmas was a nice, lightweight, aluminum stepladder so I could put up posters.* "
>
> BETTY HEARNES

But Betty stayed, and on primary night, Warren Hearnes staged what was called "The Political Upset of the Decade." He won the Democratic nomination by 51,000 votes. Warren had taken the lead early in the contest and except for one brief period, held onto that lead the entire night. Although Bush came on stronger in his home of Jackson County than anticipated, Warren's strength in St. Louis City and County was overwhelming.

Upon the Hearnes' return to Southeast Missouri, a caravan of 100 cars escorted them from the Sikeston Airport to Charleston where over 1,000 people gathered to hear Warren's heartfelt thank you for their support, followed by a 400-guest reception in his honor.

The grand prize, the Governor's office, was within striking range because normally winning the Democratic primary in Missouri at this time meant winning the office. But Warren and Betty would leave nothing to chance. They continued to endure 20-hour-a-day campaigning to defeat the

Republican challenger, Ethan A. H. Shepley, a St. Louis attorney and former Chancellor of Washington University.

At the same time, they worked to mend fences, unify the party once more, and assume the leadership of the party banner. Warren's campaign manager, Delton L. Houtchens of Clinton, was named Democratic State Chair, to assume the reins of the party machinery. At the Democratic National Convention in Atlantic City, Missouri staged a parade on The Boardwalk with Warren and Governor John Dalton, a Bush supporter, leading the procession in a miniature Model T Ford as a symbol of party unity. The body language of the two expressed a closeness neither man probably felt since they were squeezed together in the only seat of a car that was just 20 inches wide.

The following month at a Democratic rally in Jefferson City before 2,000 party faithful, Warren assured state workers who had backed his opponent in the primary that if he became Governor, all he expected from them was "the same loyalty they gave to Governor John M. Dalton."

Former President Harry Truman, another Bush supporter, began to support Hearnes publicly. Warren ratcheted down his anti-Establishment rhetoric.

Perhaps the most significant sign that the party was closing ranks came at a Jackson County Democratic fundraising dinner on Bush's home turf. Five hundred fifty people from every faction of the Democratic Party showed up to hear Warren say, "We all know there was a lot more at stake here tonight than attendance. We are like a family that chooses sides during the primary, but now the primary is over, and the family is back together again."

Even Hilary Bush finally came out in a public endorsement of Warren the month before the election.

> ❝ We've already done that. Where were you, Mr. Shepley? ❞
>
> *WARREN HEARNES*

An outstanding moment in the campaign was the debate between Hearnes and Ethan Shepley before the Missouri Bar. Although some thought Shepley's skills would best Hearnes in live debate, that was not what happened. To Shepley's repeated criticisms of state government's failure to respond to pertinent problems, Hearnes courteously replied, "We've already done that. Where were you, Mr. Shepley?" Time after time, Shepley gave him the opportunity and Hearnes queried, "Where were you, Mr. Shepley?"

The Bar Association called it "the Great Debate" but Shepley did not carry a grudge. He and Hearnes became friends and Shepley co-chaired the campaign to change the Constitution so that Hearnes could run for a second term as Governor of Missouri.

While the Democratic family was coming together, Warren and Betty were trying to keep their own family together in the midst of campaign chaos. The Hearnes had been campaigning since March, and at the same time, Betty was juggling housework, church activities, and school schedules for a sophomore, a seventh grader, and a first grader at their split level yellow brick house in Jefferson City.

"Neglecting home and children is something that worries you, and to be honest, you have to admit there is neglect," Betty said in an interview. "We try to compensate. When there's a free moment where the ordinary couple would go somewhere by themselves, we spend it with the children. And this summer they went along with us."

In spite of all the family sacrifices and political struggles, the entire Hearnes family had plenty to celebrate when the November election results were tallied. Warren had won by over 400,000 votes.

> " Neglecting home and children is something that worries you ... "
>
> BETTY HEARNES

The Hearnes household was a madhouse that night. Two phones in the kitchen and two phones in the den rang constantly—first to Hearnes' staff with returns coming in from various parts of the state and later with calls of congratulations from everywhere in Missouri. Some people were glued to the two television sets in the living room. The kitchen counter was stacked with unwashed dishes, the remnants of a rushed buffet meal everyone had gulped down. Warren was trying to freshen up for an election party at a downtown Jefferson City hotel in between taking congratulatory phone calls and reading his victory statement over the phone to news hungry reporters.

Yet in the midst of all the hoopla and pandemonium came the sinking realization. Come January, after years of planning for this moment, the dream would be fulfilled. At age 41, Warren Eastman Hearnes would be the Governor of the State of Missouri, one of the youngest men to hold that high office, and Betty Cooper Hearnes would be Missouri's First Lady.

Top left – Warren Eastman Hearnes is sworn in as Secretary of State by
Supreme Court Judge C.A. Leedy, Jr., in 1961. Lynn and Leigh Hearnes participate.

Left – In 1969, as Hearnes is sworn in for an historic second consecutive term as
Governor, Lynn, Leigh and the baby of the family, Julie, are on hand to assist.

Above – Hearnes on the campaign trail, 1968 (top) and (inset) "The Gentleman from
Mississippi," State Representative Warren Hearnes, 28, of Mississippi County, 1951

All photos courtesy of Missouri State Archives

CHAPTER THREE

Coordination, Conflict & Collaboration

*"I sure have a lot more visitors than I did
before the primary election."*

Photo on previous page –

Warren Hearnes

Portrait by Robert C. Holt, Jr. • From the Hearnes Personal Collection

The following week Warren met with Governor Dalton, who promised his full cooperation to make the transition of administrations as smooth as possible. Governor Dalton placed all his department heads at Hearnes' disposal to brief and consult with the new leaders in the Hearnes administration.

Hearnes announced that he intended to invite five Senate leaders and five House leaders to a series of budget conferences in the upcoming weeks.

One of the major news announcements by the Governor-Elect was that his inauguration would break with tradition. In the past, Governors took the oath of office in the Rotunda of the first floor of the State Capitol. Warren announced that a platform would be built on the south steps of the Capitol so a much larger crowd could attend the ceremony.

Meanwhile, at a time when Warren was trying to hire his staff, appoint his cabinet, prepare his budget, and plan an inaugural, three major incidents threatened to create problems for the new administration before Warren even took office.

Some Senate and House leaders who had supported Bush were still smarting a bit from their candidate's defeat. When some of Warren's supporters tried to stage a coup in the Senate and remove the leadership, they failed. Warren was in Florida for a brief vacation when this occurred, but he still was held responsible. It took some major diplomacy to smooth that situation over, and Warren would have to work to win over the Bush supporters in the Senate. Fortunately, the House members were strongly behind him because of all his years of service there.

A second blow struck when a Kansas City federal court held that both chambers of the General Assembly were malapportioned in violation of the one-man, one-vote rulings by the U.S. Supreme Court. The judge ordered that the Senate and House would have to be reapportioned on a population basis. In the midst of a meeting with legislative leaders on this issue,

Warren received word that a second federal court had voided Missouri's ten Congressional districts because they varied a great deal in population. Now the fear existed that reapportionment would consume the 1965 legislative session, making other accomplishments impossible.

Two staff members proved key in getting the Hearnes agenda on track in the state legislature and keeping it there—Eugene P. Walsh and Austin Hill. Walsh was a former St. Louis state representative who had been the legislative lobbyist for Jefferson City. Hill was a Howard County state representative who became House Chief Clerk and then Chief Deputy for Secretary of State Warren Hearnes. Walsh was appointed as the Governor's legal consultant, and Hill was appointed Director of the Department of Health and Welfare. These two men would prove to be a powerful tag team on behalf of Warren Hearnes' priorities.

Both men were extremely popular with extensive legislative experience. Walsh had the urban interests covered, while Hill could tend to rural issues. Walsh would represent Governor Hearnes before House and Senate committees and straighten out legal issues in legislative initiatives. Hill would visit legislative offices and win support for the Governor's programs.

Other key aides to Hearnes were Floyd Warman, who became Warren's administrative assistant after being a top coordinator for the winning campaign, and Warren's longtime assistant from his days in the House, Cathryn Adams.

However, unlike modern day gubernatorial transitions where the Governor-Elect has a budget to support a transition staff, all the work preparing for a new administration fell on Warren, Betty, Floyd Warman, and Cathryn Adams.

As occurs when power is about to be transferred from one Governor to another even today, activity in the Dalton Governor's office slowed and became next to non-existent while phone calls and activity in the much smaller Secretary of State's office down the hall increased to a fever pitch and remained there. With top appointments to be made and 2,000 state patronage jobs possibly available, everyone wanted Warren's ear. Many times people had to stand and wait in the corridor because there was no room in the office. Letters poured in at the rate of several hundred on Monday and an average of 75 on other days.

Warren's days were filled with meetings on major appointments, conferences with legislative leaders, work with legislative research staff to draft his proposals, and sessions on the state budget. To handle the flood of correspondence, Warren would take a stack of letters and a Dictaphone home with him every night to dictate replies late into the evening and then again when he awakened at 5:30 a.m. the next morning before going to work.

Therefore, it fell upon Betty and Floyd Warman to plan the inauguration, prepare for moving day to the Governor's Mansion, and compile a list of honorary colonels. The title of honorary colonel is bestowed by Governors on their loyal campaign supporters. The honor is personally costly because the colonels have to buy the dress uniform specified by the administration, and they receive no pay or stipend. However, they have the honor of marching in those uniforms in the inaugural parade as the official color guard of the Governor-Elect. Warren ended up appointing a record number to bear this distinction—750 honorary colonels. Then he broke his own record for his second inauguration with a thousand colonels appointed.

Along with planning the inauguration, the other major responsibility for Betty was to prepare the family to move from their Boonville Road home to the Governor's Mansion. After Warren's win in the primary election, Betty had graciously declined Mrs. Dalton's invitation to visit the Mansion because she did not want to take a chance of jinxing Warren's victory in the general. Now that the election was over, she was pleased to accept Mrs. Dalton's invitation to tea.

Accompanied by her sister, Mrs. Harry Warren, Jr. from Charleston, Betty went to the Mansion for a four-hour visit with Mrs. Dalton. Since it had been 24 years since a Governor with young children had lived in the Mansion, life in the official residence was going to be quite different—not to mention the Hearnes' even more lively zoo—a menagerie of pets that included Sonny, a dog of mixed ancestry Warren had bought from the dog pound for 97 cents; Yertle the turtle, a tribute to Dr. Seuss; a parakeet named Tweedie; a toy poodle named Colonel; a cat; and a bowl of guppies.

> " *I don't know what he thought he was going to do with us when he was elected.* "
>
> BETTY HEARNES

Finally, it began to sink in to Betty that she was about to assume the duties of First Lady. "I just never gave

❝ Daddy, come back here, your coat is split all the way up the back! ❞

JULIE B. HEARNES

it any thought. I don't know what he (Warren) thought he was going to do with us when he was elected," she said. "Now I feel very unworthy of the position and I wonder if I could do as well as others have done."

After weeks of frantic planning, the inaugural events began. As was the custom, Warren and Betty were entertained by Governor and Mrs. Dalton with an inaugural eve dinner comprised of country ham, chicken breasts, clam bisque, hot biscuits, and Bess Truman's famous Ozark pudding.

Inaugural Day, January 11, 1965, began for the Hearnes with a worship service at the First Baptist Church. Governor Dalton had started the tradition four years earlier. Following church, Warren changed into his formal wear for the inaugural parade and swearing-in ceremony. Not used to seeing her father in a morning coat, Julie B. stopped him as he prepared to leave by yelling: "Daddy, come back here, your coat is split all the way up the back."

The next order of the day was the inaugural parade. In keeping with another tradition, the new Governor and the outgoing Governor rode in the same car with Betty and Jerry Dalton riding in the next car. It took one half hour for the procession of more than 200 participants, including 11 bands and 750 honorary colonels, to make its way down the twelve blocks to the special platform on the south steps of the Capitol where Warren Hearnes would become Missouri's 46th Governor.

The first ceremonial acts were to swear Lieutenant Governor Tom Eagleton, Attorney General Norman Anderson, Secretary of State James C. Kirkpatrick, and State Treasurer M.E. Morris into office. Then Warren stepped to the podium to receive the oath of office from Missouri Supreme Court Chief Justice Henry I. Eager at the traditional time of high noon. However, the order of the ceremony was another break with tradition. In the past, the Governor-Elect had always been sworn in at the beginning of the ceremony. This time the best had been saved for last. While Lynn, Leigh, and Julie B. held the Bible and Betty stood by his side, Warren swore to uphold the state and federal constitutions and faithfully demean himself as Governor before a crowd of 9,000 strong.

After the oath of office was completed, gun crews of Battery D, first howitzer battalion, 128th Artillery of St. Clair, Missouri, fired a 19-gun salute across the Missouri River from the north side of the Capitol.

Finally, the moment the Gentleman from Charleston had envisioned so many years of work ago had arrived. He took the dais to deliver a new direction for the state. His inaugural address was short—only nine minutes and approximately 2,000 words—but the words made it clear that "we pledge this state to a new day."

While Warren proclaimed "this day marks an end as well as a beginning," he still promised a renewal of "that from the past which is good on which we Missourians can pattern our blueprint of government." However, the major theme of the address was the change he had stumped on throughout the long primary fight and general election campaign.

"Our challenge is to supply the morality and the know-how necessary to use the change for the common good of our citizens," Warren told the crowd.

Yet before that work began, the Hearnes administration took time to pause for an evening of inaugural celebration. Instead of the traditional one inaugural ball, three were held simultaneously—one in the Capitol Rotunda, another at the Hotel Governor, and a third at the Ramada Inn.

As is the custom to begin the evening inaugural activities, the new Governor and his First Lady led the grand march, descending the Grand Staircase of the State Capitol to review the march of state officials and their spouses and the honorary colonels who followed them. Coming down the stairs to the Grand March from the opera "Aida," the youthful new first couple made quite a spectacular entrance—Warren in his cutaway and white gloves and Betty in a gown of sapphire blue peau d'ange with a fitted bodice, hand embroidered and encrusted with crystals, rhinestones, and bugle beads.

Following the 35-minute Grand March, Buddy Kay, a St. Louis musician, band leader, and state representative (1961-1972), raised his baton, and Warren and Betty swept out on the floor to lead the first waltz of the evening. Above Kay and his band hung a picture of the new Governor. The Capitol Rotunda was decorated with green smilax and palm leaves with silver garland and stars hanging from the upper balcony.

After spending some time visiting with their guests, the Hearnes hurried on for a brief appearance at the Hotel Governor ball and then traveled to the

Ramada Inn to finish the evening at the $100 a ticket event that had been planned to refresh the coffers of the Democratic State Committee, which had been depleted by the recent campaign.

The well-earned time of celebration finally came to an end. Tomorrow the tough job of governing would begin. Earlier that day Warren Eastman Hearnes had promised Missourians "fresh ideas, fresh faces, fresh attitudes and fresh dreams." Now he would have to deliver on that promise.

INAUGURATION 1969 • Governor Elect Warren Hearnes and Betty enjoy their convertible ride in the inaugural parade that precedes the swearing-in ceremony. The Hearnes chose to have both their inaugural swearing-in ceremonies outdoors on the south Capitol lawn—a tradition abandoned in the early 1900's.

Photo by Gerald Massie • Courtesy of Missouri State Archives

"We pledge this state to a new day."

– from Warren Hearnes' Inaugural Address, 1965

INAUGURAL ADDRESS, 1965 • Photo by Gerald Massie • Courtesy of Missouri State Archives

Carolyn Smallwood, Lorraine Oligschlaeger, William Sigers, Cathryn W. Adams, Nancy Dunwiddie, Mary Sue Hemmel, Lucille Wallace, Marla Longden Matheney.

CHAPTER FOUR

A New Era–A New Style of Leadership

"I'm tired when I get home. I've been listening to problems all my life. I've heard more confessions than a priest."

WARREN HEARNES

A t first glance, the casual observer would see in Warren Hearnes a man of mild demeanor and soft spoken friendliness. While he was a man of few words, often answering press questions with a simple "yes" or "no," he was a man of deep thoughts. He would always step back to analyze the facts of each situation or issue and sift through every viewpoint before reaching a decision. However, once that decision was made, he plunged ahead—never wavering—until the goal was reached. For behind all that genteel charm was an iron will and determination of steel.

Having come from the legislature, Warren had strong bonds of friendship in both the House and the Senate, and he continued to build on that good will to accomplish his agenda. He was one of the most accessible Governors in Missouri history. He instructed his staff to keep his early morning schedule open so any legislator with a problem could see him before the start of daily session. He installed a special telephone number at his desk exclusively for legislators so they could contact him whenever necessary. He initiated the practice of holding luncheon meetings with the Senate and House floor leaders every Monday at the Mansion. At least once a month, he met with the Senate President Pro Tem and House Speaker.

When major pieces of his legislative package were being discussed, it was common to see Governor Hearnes strolling through the legislative halls, visiting legislators in their offices or joining them in post session discussions at the Ramada Inn or Hotel Governor. He loved to sit down in their offices to swap jokes and share old legislative "war stories."

Unheard of for an incoming Governor, he actually sat through all the appropriation hearings and funding appeals before setting up his budget as Governor.

From the very beginning, he set up a bipartisan environment of cooperation, always including friends from the other side of the aisle in decision making. As Governor-Elect, he directed that his budget briefings with Senate and House leadership include Republican Senator Dick Webster and Republican Representative R.J. (Bus) King. In addition to these two members of the minority party, he often sought the counsel of Senators Earl Blackwell, Robert Young, and John Downs. Dick Webster liked to tell people that when Warren came to the Republican stronghold of Joplin to campaign, it would slip Webster's mind to inform his constituents that Hearnes was a Democrat.

All of this legislative good will and popularity would ensure that Warren's first term was one of the most successful in Missouri history.

Warren also had a great working relationship with Lieutenant Governor Tom Eagleton. Eagleton liked to tell the story of sneaking a six-pack of beer into the Mansion past teetotaling Betty after work one night so he and Warren could have a chat. When Eagleton was removed as the Vice Presidential candidate by McGovern at the Democratic National Convention in 1972, he wrote Warren and Betty "two hours after axe time" as he referred to it: "You are two of the greatest. Politics isn't so bad when people like the Hearnes are in it." The Hearnes would remain close friends of Tom and Barbara Eagleton until Tom's death in 2007.

❝ *Politics isn't so bad when people like the Hearnes are in it.* ❞

TOM EAGLETON

Hearnes also had an open door policy with members of the press. While he abolished traditional press conferences, he gave media representatives top access. The press used to joke that "it's easier to get in touch with the Governor than your wife."

A typical Governor Hearnes day would begin when he left the Mansion for the office at 7:30 a.m. An atypical day could begin earlier if he had been up half the night with details of bills running through his head. On those occasions, the staff reported that he would burst into the office early in the morning, overflowing with new ideas on how to get his legislative package approved.

In the early days as Governor, Hearnes liked to walk to work. However, as people caught on to his walking habits, they would stake out places along the way to ask for a job, lobby for a bill, or seek his help with a problem. Since there was no Governor's security detail at that time, a practice used by modern day Governors and their families for protection, Governor Hearnes was left to his own devices to extricate himself from these situations. Soon it became obvious another form of transportation would have to be used. So a state trooper was assigned to drive the Governor to work.

Once Warren reached the office, Cathryn Adams would have his mail ready for review.

Warren would spend the day in meetings, appointments, and briefings, but if he didn't have a luncheon speech to give in the area, he liked to return to the Mansion for lunch.

At the end of the day, Cathryn would make certain he had cleaned his desk for the following day, and at 5 p.m., he would leave the office and usually catch a flight to deliver a speech somewhere around the state. Then once he returned to the Mansion, he would catch a few hours sleep before his day began at dawn again.

On Monday nights, Warren would usually sit and visit with his legislative friends in their offices.

On weekends, he would try to squeeze in some golf, if possible, and he never missed a Missouri Tiger football game if he could help it. Normally, on Saturday night, he would travel to an event. Sunday would begin with church, and then on Sunday evening, Warren would often fly to another event.

One of the major leadership changes that Warren made during his first year of office was persuading the legislature to approve a constitutional amendment allowing Governors to succeed themselves. Under the previous law, the only way a Governor could serve a second term was by running non-consecutively. But Hearnes knew that a Governor was basically a lame duck from his first day in office. While opponents of the proposal argued the change would allow a Governor to establish "a dynasty," Hearnes said: "I am a believer that a person who does not make a good Governor would be defeated in a try for a second term."

This constitutional change allowed Hearnes to be the first Missouri Governor to win a second consecutive term. When he ran a second time in 1968, he had the highest voter approval rating of any Governor in the United States—84%. His opponent was the St. Louis County Supervisor Lawrence K. Roos. Roos ran a hard fought campaign, but at the end of the day, he did not even carry his home county. In an election year in which Richard Nixon carried Missouri for the presidency, Warren Hearnes buried Lawrence Roos by more than 375,000 votes.

Another major change during the Hearnes administration was the Governor's office itself. The 35' by 50' oval waiting room was transformed into the Governor's office with new drapes, carpet, and upholstery and what had served as the executive office previously became the waiting room.

Because of his successful leadership style and wide spread popularity, Warren had the opportunity to meet most of the important world leaders of his day and many celebrities, including the Beatles. Artist Thomas Hart Benton was a great friend. Warren and Betty both had the privilege of meeting John and Robert Kennedy at the Chase Park Plaza when Warren was a gubernatorial nominee. They also met the Shah of Iran in St. Louis. The Apollo 11 space crew came to Jefferson City. Warren played golf with Vice President Spiro Agnew and met with President Richard Nixon. The Hearnes traveled to Japan and Ireland. Some of those encounters with important people made for some great stories.

> **Just be glad it wasn't an elephant.**
>
> BILLY GRAHAM

For example, when Warren joined Dr. Billy Graham on the platform in Kansas City for an outdoor event, just as the two men were about to meet, a bird flew overhead and made a deposit on Warren's suit to the astonishment of both men. Warren looked at the suit and looked at Dr. Graham who told Warren: "Look at it this way, Governor. Just be glad it wasn't an elephant."

When Warren traveled to Russia in 1971 with a group of fellow governors, he was talking to one of their Russian guides, and the guide asked him: "Why is it that you Americans think you are right and there is a God." To which Hearnes answered: "Look at it this way: If you're right and there is no God, we're even. But if I'm right and there is a God, you're in a heck of a shape." The Russian guide just stared at him and said: "Americans are so practical."

One of the most unexpected visits was by U.S. Senator Edward "Ted" Kennedy who made a surprise visit to the Mansion when he was flying around to garner support for brother Bobby's presidential bid. Caught at the last minute to host a lunch for Senator Kennedy at the Mansion when it was the cook's day off and groceries were low, Betty adapted. "It was summer, so we covered the dining room table with beautiful flowers from the garden and served hamburgers—lots of style, but not much food," Betty remembers. "I apologized, of course, for serving such everyday fare, but the Senator graciously replied that hamburger was one of his favorites."

One experience Warren would definitely like to forget is causing President Lyndon Johnson to lose his temper. When the 1966 election meant a huge loss of governorships nationally for the Democrats, many Democratic governors were not pleased and felt that President Johnson's poverty programs were a major drag on the election. Their displeasure was very vocally expressed during a heated private discussion about the future of the Democratic Party at a Democratic Governors Association meeting in White Sulphur Springs, West Virginia.

When they left the meeting, a cadre of reporters was camped out outside the door waiting for interviews. These members of the Third Estate asked Warren what they had discussed, and he certainly lived up to his reputation for candor and outspokenness. His straightforward and honest answer was: "The Governors agreed that if President Johnson didn't change things, they'd have to change presidential candidates in 1968." The comment made the national news and a furious President is said to have referred to Warren as an SOB.

Now when Johnson was furious with someone, it wasn't a short lived fury. So Warren and several other Governors in Johnson disfavor were summoned to Johnson City, Texas, for a dressing down. Governors Connally of Texas, Hughes of Iowa, McNair of South Carolina, and Hearnes of Missouri were all on the invitation list. The Governors had agreed to stick together and kept with their strategy as President Johnson continued to rail on them during their meeting. Warren recalls Johnson's ears turned bright red. However, when LBJ zeroed in on Hearnes for particularly angry words, Governor McNair stood up for him and said: "Mr. President, it's fair for you to know that we all felt the same way as Governor Hearnes." At that point, the situation began to cool down.

Because of Hearnes' leadership prominence on the national stage, Warren and Betty had two major opportunities to showcase Missouri to other Governors and First Ladies. In 1967, they hosted the five-day Midwestern Governors Conference at the Lake of the Ozarks. Seventeen first families and a thousand guests enjoyed Missouri hospitality that encompassed boat trips, pool parties, dancing, and a formal dinner that included vichyssoise, beef Wellington, and strawberries Romanoff.

In 1970, Missouri hosted the National Governors Association meeting for the first time in 34 years at the Lake of the Ozarks. California Governor Ronald Reagan was among the conference attendees electing Warren Hearnes as Chairman of the organization.

Throughout the eight years of his administration, Warren Hearnes developed a leadership style that was admired, envied ... and sometimes cursed ... as the LBJ incident illustrated. Yet he also remained steadfast to his principles and his personality. When he looked back decades later at the decisions the Hearnes administration made during this time period, Warren believed he was a man who kept his promises. The next few chapters will outline many of those major promises kept to the citizens of Missouri during the Hearnes years.

Governor Hearnes, with Betty by his side, shakes hands with
President Lyndon Johnson, January, 1965.

Photo by Cecil Stoughton • From the Hearnes Personal Collection

Above – Governor Hearnes with Apollo 11 astronaut Michael Collins,
followed by Buzz Aldrin.

Left – Governor Warren Hearnes enjoys the
festivities surrounding the visit of the Apollo 11
astronauts and exhibit.

Both photos by Whitey Owens • Courtesy of Missouri State Archives

Governor Warren Hearnes addresses the Japanese Assembly, Japan, 1972

FOUR MISSOURI GOVERNORS, 1965
Left to right – John Dalton, Hearnes, Forrest Donnell and Lloyd Stark.

Left to right – Texas Governor John Connally, Governor Hearnes, President Johnson and
Iowa Governor Harold Hughes, gathered for a conference in Johnson City, Texas, 1967

Hearnes with Senator Ted Kennedy, circa 1967 • Below – NY Worlds Fair, 1965, Joe Garagiola, Stan Musial, Gov. Warren Hearnes and Julius Garagnani

Both photos from the Hearnes Personal Collection

CHAPTER FIVE

Out of the Shadows

*"I know the work you are doing stands like a beacon light
on a stormy coast—
a welcome sight to one in distress."*

WARREN HEARNES

Photo on previous page –
Governor Hearnes, at work in his Capitol office.
Photo by T. Mike Fletcher, Florissant, MO • Courtesy of SBC Global

When Warren E. Hearnes stepped into state government in 1951, few could imagine the impact his career would have on the treatment of Missouri's mentally ill people. By the time Hearnes left the Governor's Office in 1973, he could look back on his achievements in several areas of care. Thanks to Warren Hearnes, the State of Missouri led the nation in supporting an effective system of state hospitals, using cutting-edge strategies to treat addiction, a state-of-the-art youth center, and a network of community mental health centers that put help within an hour's drive of any community in the state. He had also proven his humanity by ensuring that the most dangerous mentally ill, the criminally insane, had adequate facilities and a chance at rehabilitation.

At the time, it had become clear that warehousing mentally ill people for life was not a cure. Missouri's state hospitals and training schools were overcrowded, and there was little hope that the problems would go away. The Council of State Governments revealed in a study that the U.S. population increased 2.6 times between 1880 and 1940, but the population of mentally ill in state institutions had increased 12.6 times.

Indeed, this was the peak of population for Missouri's state hospitals. According to the State Manual of 1951, each of the four state hospitals was over capacity. In total, they housed an estimated 10,000 in facilities built for 8,000. In addition, the training school at Marshall housed 1,865 students in a facility meant for 1,510, and in St. Louis there were 537 students in a training school for 386, with a waiting list of 160. These schools were designated for training the "feeble-minded and epileptic."

Although a few new buildings had been constructed after World War II, the older buildings were deteriorating. Staff salaries were so low that it was hard to attract competent workers. At Hospital No. 1 in Fulton, for example, psychiatrists made from $4,882 to $5,124 per year. Those employed as Hospital Attendant I, the largest category of employment and workers with the most contact with the patients, made $1,452. These attendants stayed with patients day or night on 12-hour shifts. Doctors' benefits included housing on the hospital grounds. Many other workers also stayed on the hospital campus.

To make ends meet, each hospital owned land and equipment to raise food and to make many of the things they needed. Despite the seeming self-sufficiency, however, budget shortfall was a constant problem, and the hospitals depended on the labor of patients. One patient wrote: "Many of these patients work hard all day at necessary jobs within the hospital–kitchen, cafeteria, peeling room, mending room, sewing room, laundry, dairy barn, greenhouse, and many others. Many work at jobs that require considerable responsibility and skill. They receive no pay whatsoever for their work."

Thorazine, the first modern psychotropic drug, sedated patients.

For progressive lawmakers like Warren Hearnes, the idea of locking people in institutions seemed wasteful and unnecessary. While treatments were primitive and ineffective for the long term, the most optimistic piece of the mental health puzzle was the invention of new medications. Thorazine, the first modern psychotropic drug, sedated patients. By using it, dangerous patients could be quieted. There was also hope that Thorazine could provide therapeutic value by inducing "artificial hibernation." The possibility of treatment and rehabilitation seemed promising—if there was a legislature willing to support them.

Hospital No. 1 at Fulton was the hospital closest to the Capitol, and the first state asylum west of the Mississippi River. This facility would become the flagship of the state program. It was also the hospital in need of the most attention when Representative Warren Hearnes became House Majority Leader. A few months before he assumed his new position, the main building at Fulton was demolished by fire. The event, on March 15, 1956, was reported across the United States. No one was killed, but the historic building was lost, and many records were destroyed. Some patients, abandoned by families years earlier, became anonymous members of the system. Also lost were the cemetery records. Most importantly, the administration offices, living space for patients, and many staff apartments were in the main building. It was a time when leadership from the legislature was especially important.

The shortage of supplies and staff was acute, and the staff was underpaid and overworked. Even though the 40-hour week had been mandated, it was not until August 1, 1956, that the Hospital was able to hire enough staff to allow a 40-hour week for most workers. For attendants, the 40-hour week did not begin until October 15, 1956. The new Administration Building, completed in 1958, is still in service.

Several other problems demanded attention when Warren Hearnes became majority floor leader in 1957. On the positive side, however, Missouri's social welfare movement was in full swing. Files of the Missouri Association for Social Welfare (MASW) in 1958 show 2400 memberships of unions, caseworkers, hospitals, churches, health organizations and service organizations. With Warren Hearnes leading the legislature, MASW became a partner in pursuit of new programs and funding.

Regional Centers

Clearly, there was a need for new solutions, and Warren Hearnes was creative and energetic in finding them.

In 1959 the Division had created geographical "zones" of service for state hospitals. The large areas left people hours from help. Shortly after Hearnes' election as governor, Dr. George Ulett, Director of the Division of Mental Diseases, and Jack Stapleton, Jr., a lifetime advocate for people with mental retardation and the publisher of *The Dunklin Democrat*, called on Hearnes about a new plan. They explained to the incoming governor that they wanted to have nine regional diagnostic centers for mental health treatment, thus bringing treatment to everyone within an hour's drive. The story goes that Hearnes smoked a cigar and listened—then thanked them and winked.

Dr. Ulett and Stapleton left the office and Dr. Ulett asked, "Well, Jack, what does that mean?"

Jack replied, "George, that means he'll recommend them and we'll get it done." Get it done he did and Missouri was in the forefront of the nation after authorization and financing for nine new regional diagnostic and treatment clinics for the mentally retarded. With this man in the governor's chair, the people knew mental health had a friend.

> **"** *...He'll recommend them and we'll get it done.* **"**
>
> JACK STAPLETON, JR.

A major achievement of the Hearnes administration, these centers enabled families to find treatment within an hour's drive of their homes. They could care for family members at home rather than placing them in state facilities. This close proximity enabled mentally retarded people to participate in their own communities. To make the lives of these disabled even more meaningful, Hearnes' help was crucial in passing Senate Bill 52 (RSMo 178.900-178.930), the Sheltered Workshop Bill.

Sheltered Workshops made it possible for adults with developmental disabilities to be employed in useful work. A parent of one such adult wrote:

> "While it is true that a small percentage of the mentally retarded can be successful in the normal workplace ... the vast majority of persons with mental retardation cannot function in normal settings.

> "Nothing can replace the smiles on our sons' and daughters' faces as they work and interact with their peers in a stress-free environment. Nothing can replace their pride in a job well done."

Warren Hearnes was responsible for expanding the special education program to include emotionally and socially exceptional children, doubling the number of trainable children being accommodated and establishing 38 sheltered workshop programs.

In addition to these advantages for the mentally retarded, three intensive treatment centers were funded and opened for the mentally ill. One of the new centers was Mid-Missouri Mental Health Center in Columbia, opened in January 1967 next to the University Hospital in Columbia. Short-term treatment was an innovation at the time, and "Mid MO" was designed to serve 52 mid-Missouri counties with intensive, short-term treatment with beds for 30 children, 73 adult psychiatric patients and 17 alcoholic patients.

Until The Alcohol and Drug Abuse (A.D.A.) program, another Hearnes recommendation, alcoholics were housed in locked wards with mentally-ill patients. A.D.A. was a breakthrough program specifying 28 days in the hospital for detoxification and therapy followed by release to outpatient care in the community and follow-up by groups like Alcoholics Anonymous. The pilot program at Malcolm Bliss Hospital in St. Louis under Ulett had demonstrated that after one and two years, 60% stayed sober, 20% were drinking less, and 20% were unchanged. The center received national attention.

The Maximum Security Unit (Biggs) at Fulton serves the entire state in housing the criminally insane. When Warren Hearnes went into the legislature in

1951, the facility offered little hope of rehabilitation. There was an acute staff shortage, and the building was overcrowded. There was no room for therapies and education. For recreation, Biggs had only two "bull pens," each 75' x 125'.

Warren Hearnes saw that funds became available to improve treatment. With a new appropriation, a ward was converted into administrative offices, a staff room, and space for therapies. Employee bedrooms were turned into classrooms and a dentist's office. Spaces were re-modeled as a canteen, library, barber shop, and visiting room. The basement area, formerly used for storage, became an Occupational Therapy Department and recreational services area. A softball diamond was added to the grounds.

Biggs now had nine wards, each with a capacity of thirty-five patients. In each ward there were eleven single rooms and a large dormitory with twenty-four beds, two and four beds to a cubicle. Each ward had a large day room, a nurse's office, lavatory, and a utility and clothes room. The goal was to provide security for the public, but, at the same time, the setting had to be conducive to therapy for mentally ill people who may recover and re-join society.

In 1965, when Warren Hearnes became governor, the Biggs Building was again improved. At the time, the Biggs Building was in especially poor shape, even to the extent of having windows missing. When Superintendent Donald Peterson finally convinced the Department that he needed to rehabilitate and expand Biggs, they offered him $700,000. He said: "I told Dr. George M. Ulett ... there was just no way ... that I'd get anything for $700,000 that would be useful ... He said I'd better take it, but I said I'm just not gonna do it, George, this is a trap."

❝ There was just no way ... that I'd get anything for $700,000 that would be useful. ❞

DONALD PETERSON

Peterson asked his staff for a detailed report on Biggs for the Midwestern Governors' Conference Interstate Workshop. He passed the report to Governor Hearnes. The report included detailed plans for improvement, including a new dining hall, a swimming pool, and a gymnasium. With Hearnes' support, the building program was completed in 1968-69.

Under Warren Hearnes, there was also money for new staff. A consultant in forensic psychiatry came two days per week. Psychologists, psychiatric social workers, recreational, occupational and music therapists, chaplains, teachers, and volunteers all hoped that Biggs could move from a security-obsessed facility to one emphasizing therapy. The most effective drugs were available as soon as they had proven their worth. In the words of one worker, "It is indeed surprising to see how much can actually be done for the so-called criminally insane patient ... if one has a well-planned organized program and is fortunate enough to have an adequate and sufficient staff..."

The restructuring and renovation allowed Biggs to group patients together according to their treatment plans. A newly admitted patient lived in Biggs 7 or Biggs 8, wards that were isolated from the others. After patients stabilized, they were moved to a ward with more freedom, moving in the building from the top floor to the bottom. Transfers could be made without a court order, but the patients were carefully screened before moving, and the superintendent was consulted if there was any question about a move. Trustworthy patients could move to wards that participated in activities and dances and were allowed to socialize while in the dining room. They might work in a sheltered workshop or in the community, as preparation for returning home. In 1962, the program had resulted in 55 patients being discharged and in 1963 that number had risen to 62 discharges.

Some older patients, although not allowed to go home, were eventually moved to the Geriatrics Building. But the goal was for patients to make a smooth transition back into life in a community even though making that move was admittedly difficult.

Treatment of Juveniles

Another problem was a new population in Missouri's state hospitals: juveniles with severe behavior problems. Care for these youngsters became a passion for Warren Hearnes. As early as 1951, Fulton State Hospital had taken three boys under fourteen years old, and twelve boys and ten girls aged fifteen to nineteen. By July 1957, the population of eight- to sixteen-year-olds had stabilized at around 20 juveniles and the hospital reported that they were curtailing admission of children because of lack of space and staff.

With Hearnes as Floor Leader in the General Assembly, there was the possibility of building an effective treatment plan for these children, so

Hospital No. 1 established a children's unit in 1957, setting the quota at 20 children. In 1958, the Children's Code commission re-wrote the Children's Code, providing for individual treatment, including psychiatric treatment, for children and adolescents under seventeen-and-a-half years old.

By 1960, there were 90 children at State Hospital No. 1, and by 1962, there were 175 children and adolescent patients under seventeen-and-a-half years old living in a building that dated back to the Civil War. Some were delinquent but others came to Fulton as neglected, abused, abandoned, or children who could not adjust in foster homes. In 1963, there were 106 boys and 45 girls admitted, and 76 discharges.

One juvenile later wrote about being in the system as an eighteen-year-old. In the admission ward, there were 30 patients ranging from a ten year old epileptic to a seventy year old man with depression. When juveniles were admitted, therapies included individual and group psychotherapy, play therapy, psychodrama, recreation, occupational therapy (O.T.), crafts, music therapy, dance therapy, hygiene, religious discussions, church services and ward meetings.

In 1968, the General Assembly appropriated $3,800,000 for construction of the Warren E. Hearnes Children and Youth Center at Fulton, a six-building complex with residential units, schools for high school and younger children, a gymnasium, recreational center, and administration building. Besides serving juveniles, it would become a training center for University of Missouri students studying child psychiatry and special education.

Dedicated in 1971, the Center took referrals from juvenile courts, schools, parents, and other agencies. The age limit was thirteen to sixteen years old, with 30 beds for female patients and 45 for males. Age rather than disability was the defining factor for residents of the Hearnes Center, so by 1976, the population included a variety of juveniles with disabilities that ranged from retardation and autism to violent delinquents.

Despite the challenges of working with juveniles, the staff felt they had backing from Governor Hearnes to accomplish great things. One worker remembered:

> That campus was ideal ... all one story ... air conditioned. Back in the education building, we had a full auto repair shop to teach the kids auto mechanics. There was a TV studio ... That was kind of the seat of filming things for the Department of Mental Health ... It was like a

little community almost. In addition to the three inpatient wards, we
had a very large, active children's outpatient service ... a day treatment
program for the younger kids.

Children as young as three or four came to the Center, and there was money
to take the kids on outings to Six Flags and other places. Most importantly for
the success of the new programs was training. One 22-year-old aide started
work at the hospital in 1971 and built a lifelong career at the hospital. Her
preliminary training at the hospital took six months, and the classes included
anatomy and physiology, medications, psychology, and the study of patient
interaction.

"Hearnes" soon became well known for its multi-disciplinary approach.
With the end of the mass admittance ward, a staff member boasted that,
"Within 72 hours of a child's arrival at the Center, he receives a diagnostic
evaluation by the multi-disciplinary team."

An initial, individualized program was designed for the child to meet his
emotional, social, physical, and special educational needs. Psychotherapy,
both individual and group, psychopharmacology therapy, education which
included vocational education, activity and occupational therapies, speech
therapies, etc., and all the representatives of the different disciplines worked
in a team fashion to provide the desired treatment for the patient.

The treatment goal was to discharge patients back to their family and
community, but other placement was often considered–to foster homes,
group homes, or the Job Corps.

The youth center was divided into three wards. In the admission ward, the
youth stabilized under staff observation. A second ward housed children that
needed supervision, but who could earn points to go to activities. Living in
the open ward, some residents went to Fulton public schools. Clearly, The
Warren E. Hearnes Children and Youth Center was a jewel of a facility.

Summing up the difference that Warren Hearnes made in the care of
Missouri's most helpless citizens is no easy task. At the end of his service,
Missouri could be proud in its support of mentally ill citizens. All the best
treatments were available to them, and the staff was adequately rewarded
and proud of their work. Were all the problems solved? No. Each generation
will have its own challenges. But if future lawmakers work as hard and
accomplish as much for our less fortunate citizens as Warren Hearnes did,
our destiny will be in good hands.

During the terms of Governor Warren Hearnes, the budget for mental health care rose from $25.7 million to $84.5 million. He inspired a prototype treatment center for juveniles and created the nation's first intensive, short-term treatment programs including treatment for substance abuse with follow-up in the community. Most important, Hearnes had changed the state's mental health policy from custodial care to a policy of rehabilitation. This released pressure on facilities so that an estimated 50,000 patients were receiving care in their communities rather than 10,000 confined in state institutions.

The Hearnes record in mental health care was a true expression of social justice in action and has made a huge difference in hundreds of thousands of Missouri lives.

Bronze dedication plaque

From the Hearnes Personal Collection

CHAPTER SIX

A "Real Education Governor"

"...education is one of the foremost responsibilities of state government, and it is the key to advancement and progress for all our citizens."

WARREN HEARNES

Photo on previous page –

Governor Hearnes at the Proclamation of the School for the Deaf, 1965.

From the Hearnes Personal Collection

E very politician who has ever had a glimmer of ambition to become Governor pledges to be "The Education Governor." All politicians who become Governor tout initiatives as "The Education Governor." However, the reality is that only teachers and administrators themselves—who live and breathe education…who see the improvements in the most personal of ways—can bestow the title with any degree of accuracy. That is why until Mel Carnahan assumed the office in 1992, whenever educators gathered, either formally or informally, for two and one half decades, only one Governor was ever referred to as "the last 'real' education Governor." That Governor was Warren Eastman Hearnes.

Warren's strong ties to education began early. In 1941, when he was a student at the University of Missouri, Warren was hired by Everett Keith at the Missouri State Teachers Association. Warren's job was to wrap and package books, for which he was paid 35 cents an hour. The salary may not have been much, but the friendship with Keith lasted a lifetime.

Warren's job was to wrap and package books, for which he was paid 35¢ an hour.

Ten years later when Warren was sworn in as a State Representative, one of the first visitors to his office was Everett Keith. Hearnes introduced all the legislation for the Missouri State Teachers Association for the next year.

In 1951 and 1952, when few people understood the needs of the schools or even were interested, Warren was the leader in the House in the battle for additional funds and educational improvements. After all, Warren knew from personal experience how poorly paid teachers were. While he was a member of the legislature and attending law school at the University of Missouri, the Hearnes family was forced to rely heavily on the meager salary of Betty, who worked as a music teacher in Sikeston. He knew firsthand how minimal the retirement benefits were. He also had the opportunity to see for himself how overcrowded the classrooms were—some with 35-40 students in a class—and he realized what an adverse effect that large classes had on students' ability to learn.

Therefore, as a first term Representative, he refused to be swayed from his strong positions on education, even when confronted by overwhelming opposition. From the beginning, he remained a consistent and aggressive champion of public education. As a result, the early Fifties saw an awakening to the financial needs of public schools.

In his first session in 1951, Warren tied up the state legislature by insisting that they add $20 million more to education appropriations. An increase like this had never occurred before, but Warren knew education badly needed more than the one-third of the general state revenue appropriated, and he was ready to fight for it. A great majority of the House members soon followed his direction in spite of vigorous opposition from House Speaker Roy Hamlin.

"That young whippersnapper is going to break the state."

UNNAMED SENATOR

The Senate refused to approve the appropriation and asked the House for a conference committee. Of course, the conference members from the Senate were opposed to the increase, and four of the five House conferees were opposed because they had been handpicked by Speaker Hamlin to uphold his position. This left 27-year-old Representative Warren Hearnes all alone.

The conference committee disapproved the additional appropriation by a vote of 9-1 and sent it back to the two chambers for concurrence. Nevertheless, the fight was just beginning. Hearnes stood and with fiery fervor asked the House not to approve the action and request a further conference. The House stayed with Hearnes. They stayed with him through 20 different conference committees. Finally, the logjam broke, and the two chambers agreed to add $7 million in funding above the constitutional one-third. This was a major breakthrough for education.

Upon the final adoption of the conference report, one Senator was overheard saying, "That young whippersnapper is going to break the state."

Another early fight to the finish for Hearnes came when he discovered the appropriations for teachers were designed to give men a $300 increase and women only a $100 raise. Hearnes kept up the pressure until women received their fair share. From that day forward, men and women teachers were treated equally.

In 1952, he was one of the leaders who worked to establish the medical school at the University of Missouri in Columbia. When Warren and others began their struggle for the new facility, it only seemed to be a dream. But they succeeded, and Central Missouri has benefited ever since.

Then in 1953, Warren helped sponsor House Bill 14, improving the Public School Retirement System of Missouri. Again, in 1957, as Majority Floor Leader, he was one of two sponsors of House Bill 34, handling the bill himself before the House. This measure made Missouri's public school retirement system one of the best in the nation.

When the original school foundation program, the main source of public school funding, was passed in 1955, the measure was actively supported by Hearnes. Later in the 1958 special session, Hearnes handled a Committee of the General Assembly appointed to study the school foundation formula. The committee's recommendations led to the 1959 improvements.

Thus, when Hearnes assumed the Governor's office in 1965, he had the background and the credentials to move education forward. At the same time, several developments at the state and national levels in higher education were taking place to help Hearnes make progress with his new educational priorities.

Missouri had just adopted new laws governing the creation of community college districts and replacing the old system of junior colleges. At the national level, community colleges experienced tremendous growth. For several years in the Sixties, a new community college was being created at the rate of one per week. Missouri was creating new community college districts as well, and Governor Hearnes made state funding available to ensure their growth.

Several years prior to the Hearnes administration, the state had created the University of Missouri system. A brand new campus was created in St. Louis. The campus in Kansas City was greatly expanded. The School of Mines and Metallurgy in Rolla was restructured to be the fourth campus, joining the flagship campus in Columbia.

Careful planning and the commitment of fiscal resources were essential to making this new system a success. Newly-elected Governor Hearnes made that commitment, and he fought for the University of Missouri his entire political life.

For example, he was the champion for the Columbia campus to build a multi-purpose building. Having gone to school in Brewer Field House, he realized the University would never build a successful basketball program or athletic program if they did not have a better facility.

On a visit to Illinois, he was greatly surprised by the university's multi-purpose building and the quality of its athletic facilities and classroom space. So when he returned to the State Capitol, Warren called University of Missouri Coach Dan Devine. He asked Coach Devine why Missouri didn't have a building like the one in Champagne, Illinois. Devine answered, "Well, Governor, we asked for it, and they put it on the priority list at number 24."

❝ *It just moved to number one.* ❞

WARREN HEARNES

Hearing this, Hearnes replied, "It just moved to number one."

After a hard fight in the General Assembly, the money was appropriated, and the building constructed.

During his campaign for Governor in 1964, Hearnes had also promised he would elevate the junior colleges in Joplin and St. Joseph to four year college status. During his first legislative session in 1965, Missouri Western State College and Missouri Southern State College both became reality.

As Governor, he fully funded the University of Missouri at St. Louis and the University of Missouri at Kansas City. He created a college scholarship program for qualified needy students to help assure access to higher education. Under Hearnes, appropriations for junior colleges became based on $400 per student, instead of the previous $200, with the total funds rising from $1.6 million to $14.6 million—an increase of 812%. This fostered the development of five new junior college campuses. Student enrollment at junior colleges increased by 18,000.   He also increased the staff of the Coordinating Board of Higher Education and helped the state access millions of dollars in higher education construction money.

During the Hearnes administration, appropriations for higher education rose from $47.5 million to $144.7 million—an increase of 204%. Thanks to these efforts, an additional 36,000 students were able to attend college.

Vocational education was another area that benefited from major reform during the Hearnes administration. At the national level, the first major vocational act to be enacted in years was passed in 1963, providing much needed federal support for vocational education. Hearnes commissioned Lieutenant Governor Tom Eagleton to lead a panel to study the best way to improve vocational education at the secondary level. The panel hired Dr. Gordon Swanson, a nationally recognized expert, to conduct the study.

A report was issued known as the Swanson Report. This report proposed that certain high school districts would send students either mornings or afternoons to the area school for specific vocational training. This would make new educational opportunities available statewide.

Governor Hearnes sent a recommendation to the state legislature to implement the program. As a result, 31 area vocational schools were created. Under Hearnes, state funds for vocational education increased from $856,000 to $8.8 million—an increase of 933%.

Today, Missouri has 39 vocational education schools. These area schools have partnered with community colleges to provide 58 sites where a high level of training is available to secondary and post secondary students. Industry has the advantage of being able to train and re-train workers in manufacturing and other technologies at these sites.

Yet with everything he did to improve higher and vocational education in Missouri, Governor Hearnes pushed just as strongly for elementary and secondary education. He became the champion of public schoolchildren.

State aid for public schools during the Hearnes administration grew from $145.5 million a year to $389.2 million annually—a 167% increase. These additional state funds were needed to provide for increasing student enrollment of 147,000 and to pay steadily increasing salaries for teachers, including 13,000 new teachers hired during the Hearnes years.

Had increases in state aid not been implemented, local property taxes for Missourians would have skyrocketed.

Along with funding increases, the school foundation formula was revised. Public schools in rapid growth areas received their state aid on the basis of estimated current attendance rather than actual attendance from the previous school year, as had been done in the past.

A major change was made in the formula itself as well. A specific percentage of the formula money going to the local school district had to be placed in a Teachers Fund that could only be used for teachers' salaries. This action was a gigantic step forward in recruiting and maintaining good teaching staff.

Expansion in state aid also made it possible for kindergarten programs to operate in every school district in the state. The state's special education program was expanded to include emotionally and socially exceptional children. The handicapped students' program was improved to double the number of trainable children being accommodated, and 38 sheltered workshop programs were established.

No one was ever in a position of Missouri leadership before Hearnes that had the environment and the will to do more for education, and he always used that leadership position to reflect his genuine interest and concern for education. Many times Warren had to take unpopular stands to produce additional funds for education, but he never took the easy way out. He always stood up for the teachers and schoolchildren and took the blows from his opponents.

Warren Hearnes commanded all the resources at his disposal during his eight years as Governor to advance education at all levels, truly earning him the title among the education community as "The 'Real' Education Governor."

The Hearnes Multipurpose Building at the University of Missouri at Columbia. • From the Hearnes Personal Collection

The Groundbreaking Ceremony at Missouri Western State University in St. Joseph.

During Governor Hearnes' administration, *funding for junior colleges increased 812%, appropriations for higher education rose 204%, and vocational education funding increased 933%.*

State aid to public schools grew 167%, with revisions to the funding formula that designated a specific percentage to teacher salaries.

The Public School Retirement system became one of the best in the nation.

These changes meant better quality education and more opportunity for Missouri students.

At the podium, William F. Enright, Jr. Marvin Looney is in the dark suit directly behind him. Governor Hearnes is right of Looney and Sen. John Downs is far right beside the Governor.

From the Hearnes Personal Collection

PICTORIAL

We are deeply grateful to the photographers whose work is shared here.
These pictures make this memoir especially meaningful.
Where possible, we have credited the photographers.
We regret any inaccuracies or omissions.

Photos are in random order.

Governor Hearnes and First Lady Betty at the Mansion, 1971

Courtesy of Missouri State Archives

Left – The unmistakable profile of Bobby Kennedy is to the left of Governor Hearnes in this early 1968 photo in Washington, D.C.

From the Hearnes Personal Collection

INAUGURAL GRANDSTAND, January 11, 1965 • Left to right – Secretary of State James Kirkpatrick and Mrs. Kirkpatrick, Mrs. Norman Anderson and Attorney General Norman Anderson, former Governor John Dalton and Mrs. Dalton, Governor Warren Hearnes, First Lady Betty C. Hearnes, Leigh Hearnes, Mrs. M. E. Morris, Auditor Haskell Holman, Lieutenant Governor Tom Eagleton and Mrs. Barbara Eagleton, Mrs. Holman, Mrs. M. E. Morris, wife of Treasurer M. E. Morris.

Photo by MO Division of Employment Security • From the Hearnes Personal Collection

The Hearnes girls made state history with this prize–a photo with the Beatles prior to their appearance at Busch Stadium in St. Louis in 1965.

Left to right – Paul McCartney, unidentified guest, George Harrison, Lynn Hearnes, John Lennon, Julie B. Hearnes, Ringo Starr, Leigh Hearnes, and Rita Howe.

From the Hearnes Personal Collection

Oregon Governor Mark Hatfield, President Harry S Truman, North Carolina Governor
Terry Sanford, and Governor Hearnes at the Harry S Truman Library.

From the Hearnes Personal Collection

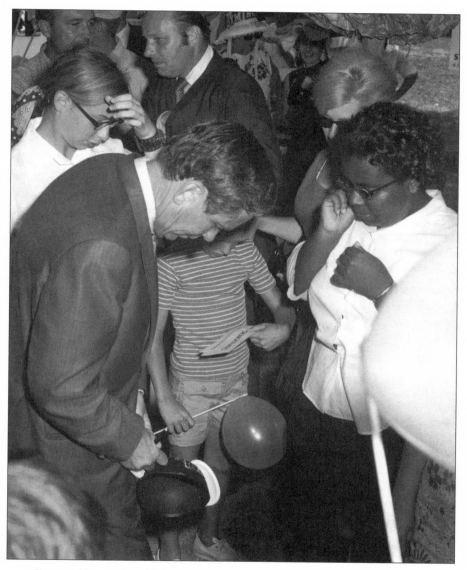

Governor Hearnes signs Mickey Mouse ears for a young supporter at the Symington for U.S. Senator/Democratic headquarters booth at the State Fair in August, 1966. State Department of Agriculture Commissioner Dexter D. Davis is in the background.

Courtesy of Missouri State Archives

Left – Governor Hearnes and Joe Garagiola in this *St. Louis Post-Dispatch* photo.

From the Hearnes Personal Collection

Hearnes, center left, at the White House with the delegation of Governors
just returned from the Soviet Union, 1968.

All photos from the Hearnes Personal Collection

President Nixon and Governor Hearnes,
Philadelphia, Pennsylvania, October 1972.

Governor Hearnes gets an affectionate pat on the head from a hospitalized youngster.

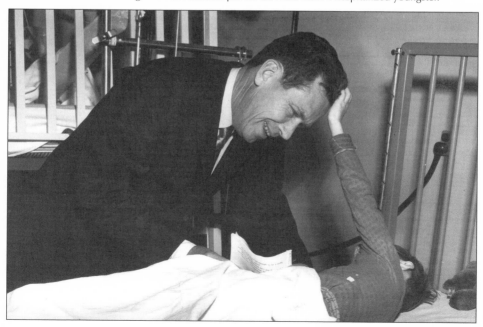

Governor Warren Hearnes with Vice President Hubert Humphrey in 1968.

From the Hearnes Personal Collection

Left top – Governor Hearnes signs legislation creating the State Archives to maintain and preserve Missouri's official documents and records. Alec Petrovic, far left, was a leader in keeping this important issue in front of legislators until it became law.

Left bottom – The Governor pays his way into the Missouri State Fair, 1965

Both photos courtesy of Missouri State Archives

Governor David Hall, Governor William Milligan, Premier Kosygin of Russia, Governor Warren Hearnes, and Governor Luis Ferre of Puerto Rico. Governor Hearnes led a delegation of U.S. Governors on a U.S.S.R. fact-finding and diplomatic tour.

Left – Governor Hearnes with West Point cadets, October 2, 1971, West Point, New York.

Courtesy of U.S. Army • Sp-4 Stoddard, Photographer

Below – White House briefing on the U.S.S.R. trip. Governor Hearnes is far right beside President Nixon whose back is to the camera as he addresses the group.

Top and bottom photos from the Hearnes Personal Collection

Governor Hearnes with Missouri mules at the State Fair in Sedalia.

Stan Musial and Warren Hearnes sign autographs in Jackson County during the gubernatorial primary campaign, 1964.

From the Hearnes Personal Collection

First Lady Betty Hearnes and the "First Daughters"–
(left to right) Julie B., Leigh, and Lynn–ready for the 1969 Inaugural Ball.

Above – Betty
(Cooper) Hearnes,
Missouri's new
First Lady, is well
represented at the
1965 inaugural events
by her family, gathered
here in the Governor's
suite of rooms in the
Capitol.

Left – Barbara and
Tom Eagleton
(Lieutenant Governor)
and First Lady Betty
and Governor Warren
Hearnes at the 1965
Inaugural Ball.

All photos by
Wright Studio,
Jefferson City, MO

From the Hearnes
Personal Collection

First Lady Betty and Governor Warren Hearnes descend the staircase in the Capitol rotunda during the Grand March of the 1965 Inaugural Ball.

Photo by Wright Studio, Jefferson City, MO

Left – Governor Warren Hearnes and First Lady Betty C. Hearnes, 1966

Photo by T. Mike Fletcher, St. Louis, MO

Both photos from the Hearnes Personal Collection

The Hearnes are official hosts for the Governors Conference at Lake of the Ozarks Tan-Tar-A Resort, 1970.

Below – A 1972 Birthday Party for the Governor. Left to right: Senator Stuart Symington, Senator Tom Eagleton (Vice Presidential nominee), Barbara Eagleton, Governor Hearnes and First Lady Betty. Photos by Wright Studio, Jefferson City

Above – Governor
Hearnes with Pope
John VI and Cardinal
Carberry.

Warren Hearnes with
Stan Musial at the
official gubernatorial
campaign kick-off
dinner, 1963.

All photos from the
Hearnes Personal
Collection

Hearnes Psychiatric Center, Fulton, Missouri, was established in the late 1960s.

Warren E. Hearnes Elementary School in Charleston, Missouri, was built in 1968.

Left – Hearnes Hall at Missouri Western State University in St. Joseph.

Photos at left and above from the Hearnes Personal Collection

The Governor's Mansion with its original brick facade exposed, a facelift that Betty Hearnes undertook while she was Missouri's First Lady. She helped the workmen hose off the shrubbery that surrounded the Mansion every afternoon after the chemicals had been used and she vacuumed twice a day during the renovation to keep the fine sand from accumulating indoors. • Courtesy of Missouri State Archives

1967 Portrait
of the First Family

Betty was proud of the Mansion restoration and preservation accomplished at her behest and, quite often, with her hands involved in the work.

She was particularly proud of having had the two Mansion pianos refurbished and made central attractions of the home.

And it *was* very much a family home during the eight years they occupied the "People's Mansion."

Left to right –

Lynn, Betty, Warren, Julie B. and Leigh

Photo by Wright Studio
Jefferson City, MO

From the Hearnes
Personal Collection

Warren with Danny Thomas.

Below – Warren and Betty with Lawrence Welk.

Both photos from the Hearnes Personal Collection

Governor Hearnes in the Executive Office • Photo by T. Mike Fletcher • Courtesy of Southwestern Bell

The Hearnes family on Warren and Betty's 55th Wedding Anniversary.

From the Hearnes Personal Collection

Left to right, front row – Julie B. Hearnes Sindelar, Andrew Sindelar, Lynn Hearnes, Leigh Hearnes Hammond; back row – Dan Sindelar, Britten Sindelar with Catherine Hammond on her lap, Warren, Betty, Clayton Hammond, and Cary Hammond.

Above – Julie B. Hearnes, 1966, plays checkers at the Mansion. Photo by T. Mike Fletcher

Left – Julie today with husband, Dan Sindelar, and their children, Britten and Andrew. Photo by Life Touch Studio

Top right – Leigh Hearnes Hammond with husband Cary and children Clayton and Catherine, 2006. Photo by Westrich Studio, St. Louis

Lynn Hearnes, Leigh Hearnes Hammond and Julie Hearnes Sindelar

Above – Family photo from 1962; at right, the Hearnes 36 years later, on the occasion of Warren and Betty's 50th Wedding Anniversary in 1998

Left to right – Leigh, Warren, Lynn, Julie, and (seated) Betty.

Photo by Westrich Studio, St. Louis

Governor Hearnes greets President Bill Clinton as he makes his first campaign stop after winning the nomination for a second term.

Right – Betty and Warren greet the rest of the campaign entourage – Vice President Al Gore, Hillary Clinton and Tipper Gore, Cape Girardeau, 1996.

From the Hearnes Personal Collection

CHAPTER SEVEN

Programs and Progress

"The duties of the office are as diversified as the state itself, and the most challenging issues encountered are those for which there is no precedent."

WARREN HEARNES

Photo on previous page –

Governor Warren Hearnes with President Richard Nixon, 1972.

From the Hearnes Personal Collection

Mental health and education were but two of the issues where action by the Hearnes administration had a monumental effect. His political and organizational skills and his longstanding relationships with other public servants on the state and national level made it possible for him to accomplish a long list of achievements in every area of state government. Hearnes liked to keep a little check list every session of his priorities, and he would check them off as the legislature sent the measures to his desk to be signed into law.

Economic Development

Just as in the other areas that shaped his administration, Hearnes' interest in economic development began during his years in the legislature. As a legislator, he was the chief author of Amendment Four, which made it possible for municipalities to issue bonds for purposes of industrial development. This act helped to attract many firms to Missouri and helped others to expand.

In his opening address to the legislature as Governor, Warren gave particular interest to the development of Missouri's natural resources into the tremendous economic and recreational assets they could be. He emphasized tourism, opportunities provided by the Federal Land and Conservation Fund Act, and the establishment of an Interagency Council for Outdoor Recreation. This council that he envisioned was composed of ten state agencies ranging from the University to various boards and commissions. The common bond was that all of them had a statutory or constitutional interest in outdoor recreation and the natural resources that provide it. He recommended a major budget increase of more than a quarter of a million dollars for the Division of Commerce and Industrial Development, which would later become Economic Development, and the legislature approved it.

With that thought in mind, Warren devoted a great deal of time during his administration to developing that keystone. He helped to bring

Cheeseborough Pond, Scholastic, and Westinghouse to Jefferson City, the 3M Company to Nevada, Dundee Cement to northeast Missouri, Ball Bearing Company to Joplin, Lily and General Electric to Springfield, Kroger to St. Louis, the Schwitzer Division of Wallace-Murray Corporation to Rolla, the National Lock Company to Sikeston, and Proctor and Gamble to Cape Girardeau.

> **Work this out. I want it done.**
>
> WARREN HEARNES

Of course, none of these new businesses came to Missouri without a lot of hard work and sometimes complications. When Missouri was trying to attract Proctor and Gamble, at one point the parties involved were tied up in labor disagreements that jeopardized the project. Even though Warren was ill with a 104 degree fever, he called both sides together and let his thoughts be known in rather strong language. He told them, "Work this out now. I want it done!" After that, Proctor and Gamble came to Cape Girardeau.

One of his greatest achievements in this area was bringing Noranda to New Madrid. The late Gene Copeland, State Representative from New Madrid, always liked to tell the story that he and a group of county officials joined Hearnes and other state officials in flying to Canada to talk to Mr. Lumbers, CEO of Noranda.

When they reached the office, Mr. Lumbers asked to talk to Governor Hearnes alone. The two men went into the CEO's office for a long time, and when they came out, Hearnes announced, "Noranda is going to New Madrid." The competition among those wanting Noranda to locate in their communities was fierce, but whatever Hearnes said, it brought that great company to Missouri.

During his administration, Hearnes helped attract nearly 1,000 new manufacturing industries to Missouri and helped more than 1,200 existing manufacturers to expand their operations. These activities brought financial investments of more than 107,000 new jobs.

Another boon for Southeast Missouri was his help in bringing hospitals to Dexter and Sikeston. In the case of Sikeston, the highway had to be widened so the city could qualify for grant money.

Hearnes also recommended the creation of the Missouri Tourism Commission to carry out intensive promotion of Missouri. Today, tourism is big business in the state, creating new businesses and jobs and pumping money into the economy, but it all began because Warren loved the state and wanted the rest of America to know about the beauty and attractions of the "Show Me State."

Strengthening community development was another Hearnes priority for economic growth. He created the Department of Community Affairs to assist local governments in gaining technical assistance and grants for city planning, zoning, housing, sewage treatment, industrial development, and other municipal and regional projects. Regional commissions, cities, and counties received $3.8 million for developing plans to assure sound growth policies. Approximately $270 million was given to local governments for urban renewal, housing, community centers, water systems, sewage facilities, and other improvements. Hearnes brought Missouri into collaboration with other states to create the Ozark Regional Commission, resulting in the construction of $27 million in projects such as vocational and technical schools, hospitals, airports, and industrial parks.

A housing development corporation was created to foster construction of low and moderate income housing units. A landlord-tenant relations act was adopted, and the first state grants were made for mass transit and urban rapid transit facilities.

Governor Hearnes signs the bill to bring Noranda to New Madrid.

From the Hearnes Personal Collection

Local voters gained the power to enact a municipal sales tax to provide cities with a revenue source tied to economic growth while reducing their local property taxes.

Nor did Warren ignore his hometown of Charleston in his community development efforts. An area of ugly wooden shacks called "Telker Row" had existed for years along Highway 62. Poor people living there struggled to keep warm by stuffing old newspapers in the cracks in the walls and shared an outside faucet in the middle of the back yard for a water supply. When urban renewal funds became available in Missouri, no one gave Charleston much of a chance of receiving any from the Nixon administration. But Governor Hearnes went straight to Secretary of Housing and Urban Development George Romney and brought a multi-million dollar grant to Charleston. If Warren Hearnes had not taken advocacy into his own hands, these improvement projects would probably never have happened.

Health and Welfare

Better health and welfare services reached thousands of Missourians due to the efforts of the Hearnes administration. A comprehensive Medicaid program was enacted to provide physician services, inpatient and outpatient hospital care, professional nursing home care, dental care, prescription drugs, optometric care, and emergency ambulance services.

New laws were passed to require the licensing, regulation, and inspection of nursing homes. Provisions were adopted to allow the elderly to live with their families and still draw assistance. Restrictions were loosened on the amount of property seniors could own and collect benefits. Aid to the elderly was increased. More than $6 million in grant money was obtained to provide community services for the elderly. State assistance was increased for the care of tuberculosis patients at hospitals in St. Louis and Kansas City.

A work program was initiated in St. Louis City and County and Jackson County to train ADC mothers so they could get off welfare and get jobs.

The elderly and the poor greatly benefited from the new programs and expansions implemented by the Hearnes administration.

Environment

The protection and preservation of Missouri's natural resources were major concerns of the Hearnes administration. Hearnes signed the first air pollution law in the state. He saw to it that water pollution regulations were strengthened, and the Clean Water Commission was created to enforce these laws more effectively.

One of the most significant environmental actions ever taken in Missouri up to that time was the passage of a $150 million water pollution bond issue. The matching state funds provided by this bond issue led to approximately $60 million in sewage control construction projects.

To renew spoiled landscapes, Hearnes championed the adoption of Missouri's first strip mine reclamation law.

These major steps taken by the Hearnes administration would help assure a healthy environment for future generations.

Crime and Law Enforcement

Recognizing the vital importance of proper training and equipment for law enforcement officers to keep people safe, Governor Hearnes created the new State Highway Patrol Training Academy as one of the finest in the nation to provide basic and advanced training for patrol and local law enforcement. Local agencies were added to the computer system that provides access to state records and to agencies in other states. This source of rapid information proved invaluable. The uniformed strength of the Highway Patrol was increased from 500 to 750 officers during Hearnes' tenure. The state laws on drug abuse were completely revised by the administration, and extensive drug abuse education programs were enacted.

The Missouri Law Enforcement Council was also created to strengthen the entire justice system, including police, courts, corrections, and juvenile delinquency. Grants totaling more than $21 million were made to state and local government agencies to fund 1,150 projects.

The strong stance Governor Hearnes took on crime truly made a difference in making Missouri communities safer for her citizens.

Highways and Traffic Safety

Under the Hearnes administration, the Missouri Highway Commission was expanded from four to six members, assuring representation from all geographic areas of the state. Three hundred and fifty miles of new four-lane highway were constructed, and a new law was placed on the books to require annual motor vehicle inspections. Governor Hearnes also eliminated the requirement that cities pay half the right-of-way costs for highway construction within city limits.

However, one of Governor Hearnes greatest disappointments was the failure to get a major toll road network built to connect northern and southern Missouri.

"I wanted to build a toll road from I-55 to Kansas City with off shoots to Jefferson City and Rolla," Hearnes remembers. "First, I couldn't convince the legislature. The bill was declared unconstitutional—the same exact bill that was all right in Kentucky [struck down by the Missouri Supreme Court]. I took it to the people, and they voted it down, too."

Other highway and safety initiatives of the administration were more successful. Hearnes championed into law legislation requiring a mandatory breath test for drunken driving suspects. He pushed the creation of the Division of Highway Safety and provided 100 new ambulances for cities and training for 1,000 medical technicians.

These actions must have had some significant effect because traffic fatalities and injuries declined in Missouri during the last two years of the Hearnes administration in spite of more drivers and cars on the road and more miles being traveled. Economic losses due to traffic accidents in Missouri were reduced by $14 million in 1970 and by an additional $13 million in 1971.

Civil Rights

Certainly, the turbulent Sixties were a time of great unrest in the area of civil rights as African Americans fought for their rightful place in the fabric of Missouri society and sought to crumble the barriers of segregation forever.

Coming from the Bootheel, an area as deeply influenced by the South as any other section of Missouri, Hearnes was surprisingly aggressive as Governor in seeking equality for all. When one Bootheel resident was asked by a reporter how he could be for Hearnes even if Warren was from the same area when Hearnes was a supporter of civil rights, the man answered, "We don't believe him."

Obviously, the man should have believed because Hearnes signed into law the state's first civil rights law, the Public Accommodation Act, in 1965 to put an end to public segregation. He increased the staff of the Human Rights Commission from 2 employees to 35. Hearnes also signed a Fair Housing law and strengthened the Fair Employment Practices Act.

"It is with some pride that I reflect upon a series of 'firsts' in the appointment of minority races to important positions in local government, the judiciary, and various state boards and commissions," Hearnes reflected. "I am proud not for myself, or for those appointed, but proud of the fact that our state is deserting the prejudices of the past and turning toward a brighter and better future for each citizen of Missouri."

However, in spite of Warren's efforts, strife still occurred. One of the most difficult situations in his entire administration was the riots in Kansas City in 1968.

The assassination of Dr. Martin Luther King, Jr., had prompted riots in many major American cities, and Hearnes had tried to plan ahead, sending observers to other places that had undergone these struggles and making advance preparations.

On April 9, 1968, the day of Dr. King's funeral, students at the primarily black high schools in Kansas City walked out of their classes and marched toward the downtown with militants gradually joining the groups. The Kansas City Mayor met the group at City Hall to try to ease tensions, but it soon became obvious that the situation had the potential to get out of control.

Acting on the Mayor's recommendation, Governor Hearnes called out a thousand national guardsmen to Kansas City. At 12:44 p.m., when an unidentified member of the police or the crowd threw a tear gas canister, the situation ignited. By nightfall, the situation was out of control with sniper fire, Molotov cocktails, fires, looting, and violence. When dawn came, over 200 inner city businesses had been looted and 94 of them had been torched. One African American was dead, ten people wounded, and 45 injured. The police had made 175 arrests.

The second day, Governor Hearnes flew to Kansas City, arriving at police headquarters to make a public announcement for the violence to stop.

In spite of his pleas, by nightfall of April 10, the inner city was a battleground. That night, 45 arson fires were set. Authorities killed six African American men and wounded 20. Snipers wounded two national guardsmen, two firefighters, and one police officer.

Mercifully, on Good Friday, April 11, the violence ceased as abruptly as it had begun. Order was restored. But the memory of that tragic event is still a source of sadness for Warren Hearnes.

Vietnam

As with not just politicians, but with every American, Warren Hearnes struggled with the issue of the Vietnam War. Supportive at first, he gradually saw the mistakes that were being made and came to the conclusion that the war that was tearing America apart could not be won. By 1970, he was calling on the President to withdraw. But along the way, his military background and conservative upbringing put him at odds with protesters on Missouri's college and university campuses. While Missouri was fortunate to only have nonviolent protests take place, Governor Hearnes had little sympathy for the protesters and denounced their activities vigorously.

One of Hearnes's most controversial stands was against the draft system. He felt it was unfair that draft quotas were filled by those who couldn't afford to go to college and that even when a lottery system was implemented, families with wealth and influence could still find ways to keep their young men from being drafted. He referred to Vietnam as a "poor man's war."

Taxes

While Warren Hearnes kept his pledge before he became Governor not to raise taxes during his first term, by his second term, it had become evident that the needs of education and mental health, two causes near and dear to him, would go unmet without new sources of revenue. So Hearnes proposed a major tax increase at the beginning of his second term in 1969.

Although Warren was able to get the increase through the legislature by healthy margins in both chambers, his relationship was permanently damaged with those known as "The Young Turk Faction" in the Senate. Senators Earl Blackwell, Robert Young, John Johnson, and others turned against Hearnes. Insults were exchanged, and many of Hearnes' second term initiatives were stopped because of the resentment of these Senators. Senator Blackwell actually led an initiative petition drive that resulted in the tax increase being defeated.

Courageously, Hearnes brought the bill back up and garnered the votes to get the tax hike passed into law.

Hearnes was always good at giving as good as he got, and his friends-turned-foes in the Senate soon found that out as they received a strong dose of justice–Hearnes style. Earl Blackwell was removed as Senate President Pro Tem. Robert Young lost his state revenue office. John Johnson found himself redistricted into a new Senate district that he could not win.

"If I had it to do over again, I would not get into any debates with Senators," Hearnes advises. "They have everything to gain, and you have everything to lose. It's like fighting coat hangers in the closet."

Governor Hearnes makes a point during a White House meeting on Vietnam.

From the Hearnes Personal Collection

The feud over increasing taxes not only cost Hearnes support in the Senate, but public support as well.

"I had a very high rating as far as people were concerned, but I had to decide whether to support my commitments to mental health and to finance education," Hearnes says. "My approval ratings went from 79 to 53 percent, and that was hard. People did get over it somewhat when they saw the results."

Although it may have been publicly and politically unpopular, recognizing Missouri needed new revenue if the state was going to move forward and refusing to take no for an answer no matter what the cost was one of the most courageous and visionary actions of Warren Hearnes during his administration.

He did succeed in getting passed a tax plan he called "creative localism," which allowed municipalities to levy their own sales tax.

At the federal level, Hearnes joined Governor George Romney of Michigan in co-sponsoring the first resolution on revenue sharing ever adopted by the nation's governors in 1965. He had the enjoyment of seeing that concept implemented in 1972 before he left office and would see the benefits it provided for Missouri under the next administration.

Reapportionment

Coming into office as a new Governor, Hearnes had faced the decision by the courts to reject the way seats in the House of Representatives were drawn. After considerable debate, the General Assembly established a reapportionment commission.

Under the previous system, the number of rural districts in the House were larger, which proponents claimed help check powerful city interests and keep a balance between city and county.

However, the "one-man, one-vote" philosophy definitely conflicted with that view. The reapportionment commission did manage to fashion a series of compromises that allowed most rural House members to keep their seats. However, the final proposal approved by voters in 1966 did strengthen urban representation.

Agriculture

The Hearnes administration was successful in getting effective measures approved to help farmers and consumers and boost the agricultural economy as well. New regulations were adopted, and electronic testing methods instituted to obtain better quality milk and other dairy products. Revisions were made in the regulation of egg production to raise standards through strict inspection. Testing of the weights of prepackaged commodities increased by 50 percent. Hog cholera and sheep scab were eradicated. New food specifications were established at state hospitals to improve the quality and lower the cost of food.

Instead of a weekly grain summary, farmers started receiving daily market summaries covering all phases of livestock and grain to help farmers market their products.

The annual Governor's Conference on Agriculture was started to bring farming and agri-business leaders together to explore the problems and potential of agriculture. The Governor's Advisory Council on Agriculture was established to advise on state agricultural programs.

Governmental Reform

As he began his second term, Warren Hearnes was determined to instigate some form of government reorganization after wrestling with the bureaucracy of 110 different state agencies, boards, and commissions during his first four years. Many state departments had been pieced together, using the same structure since the state constitution of 1945. So Hearnes recommended the Thirst State Reorganization Commission be created by the state legislature. The commission formed and began its work in the fall of 1969.

Because of all the research necessary and the difficulty of reaching consensus, the Omnibus State Reorganization Act was not signed into law until after Hearnes left office in 1974.

Along with reducing the number of agencies, the Act took the major step of establishing the Office of Administration to oversee all the state agencies.

Another outstanding change allowed Governors to propose changes for moving and assigning state agencies and programs and file those changes with the state legislature. If neither chamber vetoed the changes within the prescribed time, the submitted plans would become law.

As a result of Hearnes' work, Missouri was brought into the 20th century for effectiveness and moderation, leaving a legacy of effective government. State agencies were realigned for increased efficiency.

Diverse Other Issues

Governor Hearnes addressed many other issues to help improve the lives of Missourians as well...new laws that cannot be categorized. He achieved extensive reform of election laws to provide greater ease in voting and more accurate counting methods. He brought in a public defender system to comply with court rulings for local representation of all accused people. He created the State Fire Marshall's office and the Missouri Commission for the Status of Women. He established the Missouri-St. Louis Metropolitan Airport Authority. He also expanded the state's merit system to include the Public Service Commission, Division of Budget and Comptroller, and the Division of Planning and Construction.

As *The Kansas City Star* summarized Hearnes' eight years: "Few would disagree that Warren Hearnes proved to be one of the most adroit politicians in Missouri history... As we see it, the Hearnes record contains some major disappointments. But they have been far overshadowed by lasting achievements that will leave a permanent mark on Missouri."

Top – Governor Hearnes speaks at Rolla's groundbreaking ceremony for the Schwitzer Division of Wallace-Murray Corporation.

Bottom – Hearnes at the Dundee Cement dedication at Clarksville, Missouri.

From the Hearnes Personal Collection

SIGNING of MISSOURI'S FIRST CIVIL RIGHTS LAW, 1965

Left to right–

Committeeman Bennie Goins, Representative John Conley, Committeeman Leroy Tyus, Representative Deverne L. Calloway, Senator T.D. McNeal, Governor Warren E. Hearnes, and Representatives Mel Carnahan (the House sponsor of the bill and House Majority Floor Leader), Harold Holliday, Henry Ross, Leon Jordan, and James Troupe.

Courtesy of Missouri State Archives

CHAPTER EIGHT

Partners In Public Service and Life

"The Mansion will be what you make it."

BETTY HEARNES

Although Missourians thought they had seen a dynamo in action when Betty Cooper Hearnes barnstormed the state to help Warren become Governor, they had only witnessed a small sample of the energy, enthusiasm, and determination she would bring to the role of First Lady. However, while she was proud to be First Lady, she had always been uncomfortable with titles. As she liked to put it, "One of the first things the Founding Fathers did was to do away with titles. Just call me Betty."

Most Missourians found that an easy request to honor because Betty never knew a stranger and was a woman with whom Missouri moms could identify. She was only 37 years old when she moved into the Governor's Mansion, and she juggled the roles of First Lady and mother to three girls.

Adjusting to these dual roles and living in such a fish bowl environment was not easy. Any family moving into the Governor's Mansion finds it to be quite an adjustment. The three young Hearnes girls envisioned the historic structure as a dream house. After all, their new home offered huge rooms, a magnificent curved grand staircase with a banister perfect for sliding, and every teenage girl's fantasy—eight different telephones.

They also had visions of no more household chores with a butler, housekeeper, maid, secretary, and chauffeur on duty. Betty soon brought them back to reality with the parental edict that each girl would still be responsible for cleaning her room just as they had done on Boonville Road.

> " Just call me Betty. "
>
> *BETTY HEARNES*

Granted, the girls did have their privacy. Their bedrooms were on the third floor, and Warren and Betty slept on the second. The spacious third floor ballroom accommodated billiard and ping-pong tables, a trampoline, and even a bowling alley. Yet, in spite of having their own floor, sometimes the activities taking place in the upper story did not escape detection downstairs. Exuberant dance moves could prompt Betty to make an unscheduled visit when those gathered for a social function below noticed the first floor chandeliers shaking.

One major down side for the girls was having no nearby playmates since the Mansion was an isolated residence. The girls were also at those sensitive ages where being viewed as different was not desirable. Leigh would often talk the chauffeur in the black limousine into letting her get out of the car before reaching school so she could walk into the school grounds like other girls her age.

Once when Julie B's first grade class was scheduled to tour the Mansion, she was quite upset that her parents had not sent a permission slip to school as was required of the other parents. The day of the event, a last minute telephone plea from Julie B made Betty realize how important it was to her daughter to be treated just like everyone else. So she sent the note.

When the class arrived at the Mansion for a tour, Julie B blended in with the rest of her class, never acknowledging her mother. Finally, when the class was ready to leave, Julie B approached her mother and said, "Thank you very much" before getting back on the bus and returning to school.

The Mansion was certainly more lively with three girls living there, but Betty did her part to enliven the staid atmosphere as well. One of her first actions as First Lady was to bring music into the house. As a minister's daughter and a college music major, Betty felt having music fill the rooms was a major priority, and soon The House on the Hill was "rocking."

As a part of this effort, the old pianos in the house, which had fallen into disrepair from lack of use and neglect, were brought out of storage. Betty found a Steinway and the Chickering and moved her own personal piano into the Mansion for good measure. The House on the Hill began to reverberate with music everywhere. Betty also kept her membership in the Morning Music Club of Jefferson City and continued to sing in the First Baptist Church choir as well as being the assistant organist. She delighted in bringing musicians from across the state to the Mansion to entertain guests.

Betty's social secretary, Marge Estes Lewis, was the perfect subordinate for she shared Betty's passion for music. She was a musician herself, and between the two ladies, the Mansion was filled with singing and the sweet sound of all kinds of instruments. This was quite a drastic change. While Governor Folk's wife, a fine musician in her own right, had started the Morning Music Club of Jefferson City in 1906, First Ladies who followed had not shared that interest...until Betty.

All the Coopers sang. With a minister as head of the family, church music was a constant. According to Cooper family lore, "Cooper babies cry until they learn to sing, and then they sing 'til they die!"

Nor was the rest of the family immune. Betty was always quick to point out that even Warren sang in the West Point Glee Club. Like most children of the Sixties, the Hearnes girls liked their music, and they liked it loud. Once the sound of the Beatles was blasting so loudly from the third floor that Warren was unable to conduct a business meeting on the second floor and had to send someone to deliver his emphatic message to "Turn that music down!"

Turn that music down!

WARREN E. HEARNES

The natural extension of Betty's personal passion for the arts was her rise to champion the arts statewide. And what better bully pulpit than the Governor's Mansion?

In 1965, she set out to see her dream come true—the creation of a state council dedicated to nurturing the arts. Many of the legislators failed to share her enthusiasm with all the pressing concerns of state. In fact, when the issue had arisen in the previous legislative session, the legislators had shown their disdain by rising as one body to sing "Home on the Range." However, they had not tangled with Betty Hearnes yet.

"It is the birthright of every child to be exposed to music, to art, and to literature," Betty declared. "They are not just for the few and the rich. The encouragement of excellence is a proper function of a democratic government."

With that opening salvo, Betty's fight for a state financed arts council began. The legislation became known as "Betty's Bill," and she used every weapon in her arsenal—including her influence with the Governor—to bring the issue to the forefront. "I had the Governor in my bedroom, and that's a pretty good place to lobby," she would joke. But in those more serious moments, she would admit, "If Warren hadn't wanted it, the bill would never have passed."

"It was quite a fight to line up the votes for the bill's passage," Betty recalls. "Legislators are more concerned with building roads, hospitals, schools—in short, guns and butter are more appealing to the legislators' constituents. The problem is always the money to go around, and everyone wants a share of the pie. In 1965, we finally got our share, and each year it's a fight."

"Betty's Bill" received national attention, and she was invited to discuss ways to gain funding for the arts before the National Endowment for the Arts in Washington, D.C. Although it appeared Missouri was about to break new ground in supporting the arts, Betty hesitated to take the national stage with her bill still unapproved.

But as the adage goes, timing is everything. Right before she was scheduled to go to the podium, Warren called to deliver the message. "Make the speech," he told her. "The bill just passed."

Betty proudly stood before the national arts community in Washington, D.C., where citizens from other states pursuing a similar goal had gathered, and she announced, "We in Missouri are concerned with the theatre and art...with bringing music and literature to the people."

The New York Times called Missouri's First Lady "the Hit of the Day."

> **❝ We in Missouri are concerned ... with bringing music and literature to the people. ❞**
>
> *BETTY HEARNES*

The result was Betty's proudest achievement and her legacy to Missouri. Missouri became the second state in the United States with a state-funded Council on the Arts...an organization that is still helping local artistic projects to thrive today across the state.

Betty's view of the Council was that it would democratize the arts and this would raise all ships—giving hopes and dreams to people deprived of these cultural experiences. The arts had been so important in her own life that it was the most important part of herself that she could share. She wanted it said of the Hearnes administration: "We gave you the chance to dream." Today, Missouri still lives its dreams through the arts because of "Betty's Bill."

The other major achievement that will always be synonymous with Betty Hearnes is preserving "The People's House"—the Governor's Mansion.

When Governor James T. Blair had come into office in 1957, he refused to live in the Mansion, finding it rat and vermin infested with worn furniture, antiquated plumbing, peeling wallpaper, and crumbling plaster. The state legislature considered demolishing it. Lacking the funds and will for a total restoration, the legislature appropriated $129,000 to exterminate, install an elevator, restore furniture, redecorate, and update the wiring.

Governor and Mrs. John Dalton continued the improvements, remodeling the two guest bedrooms, the Crittenden and Prince of Wales rooms.

Yet in spite of the improvements before the Hearnes, the Mansion was far from the showplace it is today. As Betty remarked when she viewed the worn gray carpet in the downstairs area, "It looks like a funeral parlor. With a few flowers, they could lay you out in any of the rooms."

One of the first areas of concern for the Hearnes was the roof. When one of the Hearnes girls woke up in the middle of a storm with water dripping on her face, Warren and Betty knew roof repairs were in order. Buckets were a temporary solution, scattered around the house to catch the water. Betty even missed church one rainy night in 1965. The congregation would have been surprised to learn the First Lady's absence was because she was running around the Mansion with buckets to catch new leaks.

However, when the engineers came to inspect, they discovered the roof was just one of the major problems with the house. Floors were not level and were sagging. The second floor porch was in such bad shape that it was condemned as unusable.

That was enough to get Betty's wheels moving in high gear. The planning began for a gradual, phased restoration of the Mansion to its original glow. She visited the Missouri State Historical Society in Columbia, Missouri. She talked to former First Ladies and their families. She paid visits to homes in St. Louis and Hannibal that had been built by the same architect as the Mansion—George I. Barnett.

The work began with a $116,000 appropriation from the 74th General Assembly. The slate roof was replaced, and the iron millwork on top of the building was repaired and cleaned. All the wooden cornices were replaced to duplicate the original ones. The window casements were replaced, new electrical wiring and heating were installed, and the water lines replaced.

Previous tenants had used the northwest corner of the third floor as a "junk room"—a euphemism it had started to resemble with its sagging floors, peeling paper, and disrepair. So Betty started her interior work there. The bedroom was redone as a guest room, and the ceiling and the walls were repaired. A new bathroom was installed to complete the guest wing.

Another problem for the active Hearnes family was the failure of the Blair's elevator to go to the third floor, even though Julie B. didn't mind running up the narrow third floor staircase. Although a bedroom had to be torn out to extend the shaft, the Hearnes installed a new elevator to give full access.

Part of Phase I of the restoration plan was rebuilding the back porches, which were in sad shape. Leaving the columns as they were, the workers glassed in the porches and replaced the old wooden floor with clay brick tiles. This made useful space out of the decaying porches without ruining the architectural integrity of the house.

One of the problems which disturbed Betty most was the condition of the fireplaces throughout the house. She was told they were bricked up and beyond repair. Of course, the workmen didn't know that telling Betty something was impossible was only a temporary setback. She consulted with a Mr. Forshaw in St. Louis who told her about a new gas log that looked exactly like a fire and only required a vent. When workmen began to remove the brick for these new logs, the soot and dirt were unbelievable. Betty and the workers had to clean constantly to prevent damage to the house. But the fireplaces were relined. Gas logs were installed, and new brass fenders were purchased. Once again, all seven fireplaces could be used, and the flames were convincingly beautiful. Only the front hall fireplace was not fitted with a gas log. Some years before, plumbing had been installed in its cavity. The fireplace had been destroyed in a fire that damaged it and the sliding doors near by, so it was not an original feature of the home.

Repair of the fireplaces took about three years to complete. At the start of a new year in 1969, Betty realized she only had four years to complete the restoration she had set out to accomplish.

After removing the shabby carpets in the second floor family quarters, Betty discovered the floor had been pieced, and portions were sagging. So work began on taking up the floors and installing new ones. Some of the floor joists had to be replaced. The process required the active Hearnes family to spend three months hopping on boards to navigate through the rooms. Betty recalls if Warren hadn't been totally supportive of the restoration, this major inconvenience would have been the straw that broke the camel's back.

After refinishing the floors on the second floor, the workers moved to the first floor, which was in even worse shape. Betty was amused to find that newspapers had been used to shim the floorboards, but at least those doing the work had been thoughtful enough to ensure all three metropolitan newspapers were represented. This fire hazard was removed, and the floors were replaced as similar to the original ones as possible.

Replacing all the downstairs floors made for another long time for the Hearnes to hop around on boards in the Victorian Room, the Gold Room, and the Dining Room. But the obstacle course proved worth it. Betty had talked to Governor Stark during her research, and he informed her that he had installed walnut parquet in the Great Hall. Once it was uncovered, the floor was restored to its beautiful original luster.

A gorgeous addition was also placed over the newly repaired floors in the Gold Room. When the Governor's office was renovated, a Persian rug purchased by Governor Blair had migrated from the Governor's office to the Mansion. It proved to be the perfect touch to set off the renovated room.

One casualty did occur during the first floor process. On October 10, 1969, Betty fell over a workman's saw in the darkened dining room and broke her arm.

As those who do restoration work know, as the restorations unfold, one project often leads to another. While restoring the floors, the crumbling baseboards became evident. A local craftsman set the lathe and cut new baseboards exactly like the old ones.

Addressing the exterior restoration necessary to complete the Mansion project proved to be a massive undertaking. In 1937, Governor Stark had constructed an upstairs kitchen wing on the Mansion using bricks from a demolished porte cochere on the side of the house. These bricks had come from the old stable and did not match the bricks of the house. So Governor Stark had the entire house covered in white paint, which became known as "Stark White," to give the Mansion a uniform look.

After some research and consultation with paint experts, Betty discovered the bricks could be tinted to match. This became the basis for the next facet of restoration—to strip the paint and return the façade to its original brick. However, coarse sandblasting could not be used because of the soft handmade bricks, known as "pink brick." The paint was removed with an acid wash, sprayed on and washed off with a power sprayer.

This job meant all the shrubs around the house had to be protected, and the water had to be trenched away from the house every afternoon. So about 4:30 every afternoon, Betty and two workmen washed all the shrubs and ran the water away from the house.

After as much paint as possible was removed using acid, very fine sand was used to take off the last coats. In all, the workmen removed 35 coats of white paint as well as a coat of red.

Only those who have been through the ordeal of sandblasting can understand the resulting mess. Betty and her crew had to clean the inside of the house three times a day. The sand spray would make its way into the Mansion, leaving a collection of dust on all the furnishings.

Julie, at home in the Governor's Mansion with Colonel and Tweedie Bird.

From the Hearnes Personal Collection

"Our last two months in the Mansion were the only ones we had free of dust and repairmen," Betty laughed.

After the inside daily cleaning was done, Betty and her crew would work outside until approximately seven in the evening.

Trying to keep a busy household on an even keel with all this activity and disruption was not an easy task, but the Hearnes were all troupers.

The most exciting discovery occurred when the workmen were removing paint from the woodwork. Betty liked to call this event "the found treasure moment."

One of the men called Betty's attention to nails in the window casements. Upon close examination, Betty found a hidden hinge.

"If there's a hinge, there must be shutters," she exclaimed.

Joining the carpenter, she ripped out nails, pulling the casement loose and breaking the paint seal.

"The shutters unfolded like a butterfly from a cocoon," Betty remembers.

> " The shutters unfolded like a butterfly ... "
>
> BETTY HEARNES

They proceeded to find shutters all over the first two floors of the house. Betty believes the shutters had been sealed away to provide dead air space between the inside and outside walls. In the dining room, one of the windows had door shutters indicating that it had been the walk out door at one time. Betty and her crew also found door shutters in the middle bedroom upstairs.

The work crew took sixty coats of paint off the casements and about as many off the shutters. They cleaned the brass hinges and fittings and restored the shutters and casements to their original finish.

Betty also inspected the door pockets to see if doors had been nailed away, but they were gone. So two new sliding doors were added to the dining room. Betty took the brass chandeliers apart, polished them, and reassembled them.

In the Gold Room, the men took the caps of the columns completely apart, cleaned them, and put them together again. Many layers of paint had obscured the design details.

Stripping the paint off the paneling in the dining room revealed that the plate rail was original, but that other paneling had been added in the Fifties. At one time, there had been a folding walnut wall to divide the space into two rooms, but somehow, through the years, the wall had been lost. Brass sconces in the dining room were polished. The drapes were stripped down, and red flocked wallpaper was added. Walls in other rooms were stripped of layers of wallpaper, replastered, and painted. The original front doors were stripped of nearly a century of varnish accumulation.

Betty made many changes in the furnishings as well. The Steinway piano was rebuilt, and The Aeolian Company bought a new harp. A Mansion Library was started with a collection of books given by the State Library Association and the Academy of Squires. A special bookplate was designed with a replica of the wrought iron used on the Mansion trims. A group of St. Louis women made petit point seat covers for 24 dining room chairs that depicted dogwood against a red background. Since there were only 23 existing chairs, Betty had a 24th chair made to match the others. Portraits of Missouri's First Ladies were all cleaned and restored by noted Columbia, Missouri artist Sidney Larson, who also restored the famous Thomas Hart Benton mural in the House Lounge of the Missouri House of Representatives. A table that had been used to display vegetables and fruit at the 1904 Worlds Fair in St. Louis was restored and brought to the Mansion from the Poultry Experiment Station in Mountain Grove. Betty even planted a rose garden outside.

Round tables and folding chairs were also purchased so that between the dining room and the porch, 107 people could be seated for formal dinners. These all came in handy when the Hearnes prepared to leave the Mansion with a grand 100th birthday celebration. A series of teas and coffees were held before the actual birthday party, so the new tables and chairs got a great deal of use.

It is difficult to foresee what might have ultimately happened to this historic treasure that thousands of visitors enjoy today if Betty Hearnes had not undertaken the Herculean effort, working side by side with the workmen, and Warren Hearnes had not been able to convince the legislature to make the series of appropriations that funded the restoration. Missouri can be grateful that this rescue mission took place with such passion and care.

During the Hearnes administration, Betty took great pride in making the Mansion "The People's House" for all to enjoy. In previous administrations, guests to the Mansion included party guests, members of organizations holding conventions in Jefferson City, and friends of the First Families. Betty opened the doors to the public, introducing an accelerated schedule of public Mansion tours. The new scheduling accepted small groups, making the trip to the Capital City just to tour the executive residence. A busy month saw 1,500 visitors streaming through the Mansion on these guided tours.

After one particularly busy day when 300 students had flooded through the house, all personally greeted by Betty, she overheard a chaperone say, "It looks like Mrs. Hearnes would have come downstairs to speak to us."

Betty looked at her and responded, "Lady, I am Mrs. Hearnes, and I've been here all day."

Some of Betty's favorite memories are of the schoolchildren who visited. One child wrote: "Dear Mrs. Hearnes, I like your home. I like the antics." (Betty hopes he meant to say 'antiques' since she is unaware of any antics she might have performed that day.)

Another student wrote to her to say: "Dear Mrs. Hearnes, Tell me all you know about Missouri. Tell me all you know about government. Could you get this to me by Friday? That's when my paper is due."

> **"** *Lady, I am Mrs. Hearnes and I've been here all day.* **"**
>
> BETTY HEARNES

One visiting group received a very special tour. A group of scouts was passing by one day when Warren was in the yard. They struck up a conversation, and Warren told them about Missouri government. Then he invited them inside the house and gave them a personal tour.

Two of Betty's favorite stories from her years at the Mansion involved the Trustees from the Missouri State Penitentiary who staff the Mansion. At that time, it was customary to send the men from the prison at 5:30 p.m. when the Governor was entertaining guests for dinner. With such a fast arrival, any instructions had to be short and to the point. Betty had trained the men to place the china properly when they set the tables for dinner. But one night she heard the head man repeating her instructions with his own twist. "Put these plates on this table where these bears are looking straight at you, and be very careful not to break the china," he said.

At that point, Betty came up behind him and asked, "And what will happen if you do?"

The man paused, looked out the window at the Missouri River, and said, "I'll be the second man to walk on water."

On another occasion, Betty had made a breakfast speech, raced to school for a conference, zipped back to the Hotel Governor for a brunch, and returned to the Mansion for a meeting. As she walked in the door to give the butler an out of breath greeting, he said, "Boy, Mrs. Hearnes, you got a lot of prestige, but I sure wouldn't trade places with you!"

Betty got quite a kick out of the fact that a prisoner wouldn't want to trade places with the First Lady of Missouri.

However, that day was just typical of Betty's schedule. As a speaker, she was much in demand. One month she recalls speaking at 27 different events, ranging from teachers and servicemen's wives to political gatherings.

Along with the Trustees, the Hearnes administration also had another source of support staff at the Mansion. After several incidents where passersby walked right into the Mansion and up to the family living quarters on the second floor, security was beefed up. Highway Patrol officers joined the Mansion watchmen in seeing to the safety of the First Family. Today's First Families have a round-the-clock Highway Patrol security detail, but the whole movement in that direction started with the Hearnes.

Betty Hearnes had entered the Governor's Mansion with apprehension, afraid it would never become a home for their family. But after eight years of living there and all the time and care she put into restoring it and opening it up to the public, she left with some sadness. But she could also leave with a great deal of satisfaction, for her legacy to the Mansion and to the arts still lives today.

In 1968, Mary Grace Bryant of the Salem Post and Democratic Bulletin summarized the public service of Betty Hearnes beautifully when she said: "As we were leaving, the last reminder of the Mansion and its gracious mistress was found underfoot: the green woven doormat. It said simply MISSOURI. And as we drove away, I caught a final glimpse of the stately structure with its Captain's Walk topping the highest of those 27 rooms, and I thought of that word on the doormat. Just MISSOURI. Not the Warren Hearnes, not the Executive Mansion, not even Jefferson City, but simply

MISSOURI. Surely that doormat's one word benefits Mrs. Hearnes who serves not the political expediency of high public office, nor serves solely the Capital City itself, or any other special locality—but she serves simply and wholly MISSOURI."

Betty Hearnes left the Mansion in 1973 after eight years as Missouri's First Lady, but she has never forgotten that mission. She has continued to serve Missouri in countless ways ever since.

The "Stark White" Governor's Mansion, before the original brick was exposed.
(See color photos in Pictorial Section for the Mansion exterior after the renovation.)

Photo by Gerald Massie • Courtesy of Missouri State Archives

Betty and her social secretary, Marge Estes Lewis, had more in common than mutual respect–both were accomplished musicians, using every opportunity to fill the Mansion with the sound of music.

Governor Warren Hearnes and First Lady Betty pose for this portrait
on the stairway in the Mansion, 1972.

Photo by Wright Studio, Jefferson City, MO

Both photos from the Hearnes Personal Collection

The curving stairway has always been an attractive Mansion feature.
In this *St. Louis Globe* photograph, Julie B. dusts the banister as she zips to the
main floor from the family quarters above.

Left – And the stairway made an impressive backdrop for bride Lynn,
who was married at the Mansion in 1970.

Both photos from the Hearnes Personal Collection

Betty's official duties as First Lady included a few exciting opportunities to travel, such as this trip of governors and their wives to Ireland where they were received by President de Valera (1970).

Left to right – Mrs. William Cahill, Mrs. John Dempsey, President de Valera, Mrs. David Cargo, Mrs. Warren Hearnes; (back row) Mr. Moore, U.S. Ambassador to Ireland; Governor Warren Hearnes; Governor David Cargo, New Mexico; Governor John Dempsey, Connecticut; Governor William Cahill, New Jersey; Governor Warren S. Knowles, Wisconsin.

CHAPTER NINE

Readjustments

*"I have to be doing something,
and I can't join the coffee circuit."*

WARREN HEARNES

Photo on previous page –

Warren and Betty Hearnes returned to Charleston in 1973.

From the Hearnes Personal Collection

A t age 49, Warren Hearnes returned to his home in Charleston. For the first time since he began in politics, his life was not strategically planned.

"I planned my life for 22 years," he said. "I won't do it anymore. I hope we'll be happy, but we'll have to wait and see what happens. It will be a difficult period of readjustments."

Politics had not made him a wealthy man. He had a $50,000 home that he had built in Charleston six years earlier. He owned a small farm in the area and approximately $10,000 to $15,000 in personal items.

"The only thing I'll have in the bank will be my last paycheck," he quipped.

❝ *I hope we'll be happy.* ❞

WARREN HEARNES

The home place would certainly be much quieter. Only Julie B. would be returning with Warren and Betty. Leigh was in college, and Lynn had gotten married in 1970 at the Mansion. While the ceremony had been a private one, between 600 to 700 people had attended the reception.

Warren joined a St. Louis law firm as a partner and commuted there three days a week, devoting the other two days to his law practice in Charleston.

Unfortunately, at the same time, a shadow fell over Warren Hearnes—a shadow that would haunt him for the next four years. One week after leaving office, Warren received a phone call from the IRS that he was the subject of a tax investigation and that he needed to furnish the agency with all his tax records. What followed were two years of innuendoes and rumors leaked to the media that Warren Hearnes was under federal investigation.

Hearnes has always maintained that this investigation and the resulting rumor leaks were linked to preventing him from continuing his political career. After all, he had been one of the nation's most popular Governors, and in 1972, when Senator Edmund Muskie of Maine was running for President, Warren had been promised the post of Secretary of Transportation, even though there were some news reports that he was being considered for the vice presidential slot.

❝ They told me to bring everything since I graduated from law school. ❞

WARREN HEARNES

Later, Warren would discover that the federal government was interested in more than just his tax records. His entire public and private life was put under the microscope. The investigation was directed by a Republican U.S. Attorney in Kansas City, but Hearnes could never get the authorities to tell him what the point of the investigation was.

After two years of dealing with this issue, Warren took the unusual step of voluntarily asking to testify before a federal grand jury to clear his name.

"They told me to bring everything since I graduated from law school," remembers Hearnes.

Warren testified before the grand jury for three days. His brother-in-law Bob, who was the CPA that did his taxes, met with Warren. In this case, Warren was glad that Bob had insisted on meticulous records all those years.

Willard Reine, who was Warren's law partner, said when they questioned Hearnes' honesty he was reminded of seeing Warren's book of accounts where he had even listed a notary fee of 50 cents on his income.

After his testimony before the grand jury, Warren requested copies of all documents relating to his case under the federal Freedom of Information Act. His suspicions about the motivations for the investigation were confirmed when he received a copy of a letter from Alexander Butterfield, Deputy Assistant for President Nixon.

"We have [the copy of] a letter before I left office from the White House to [FBI Director J. Edgar] Hoover asking for a complete investigation of Hearnes," he explains.

Ultimately, Warren was officially cleared of any wrongdoing in 1977 by a Democratic U.S. Attorney, and he won a libel suit against the *St. Louis Post-Dispatch* for some of the negative and unsubstantiated coverage they had printed about the investigation. Nevertheless, being under that cloud of suspicion had damaged his future political ambitions.

"I don't care if you get a clean bill of health," Warren said. The grand jury "nightmare" put an end to his political future.

He entered the U.S. Senate race in 1976 as one of four primary candidates. U.S. Representative Jerry Litton from northwest Missouri was the winner, but Litton and his family were tragically killed in a private plane crash on primary election night. The task of electing another candidate was the job of the Democratic State Committee. They picked Hearnes, but election night the winner was Republican John Danforth.

After his loss, Warren left the law office in St. Louis and confined his practice to Charleston. It was not easy to start over, but he did. He recalled people were a little skeptical at first and called him a "big city lawyer."

However, Betty and he found their place in the community and continued to work.

Sadly, there were more political disappointments ahead. In 1978, Warren was unsuccessful in an attempt to run for State Auditor. He was also unsuccessful in a run for Circuit Judge. He had been appointed to the position by Governor Joe Teasdale and had been serving in that capacity. But when the election time rolled around, three people from Mississippi County filed and more from Scott County. Mississippi County didn't have enough votes to overcome Scott County. Still, as the seasoned political veteran he was, Warren rolled with the punches.

A bright spot did occur when a state representative seat opened up in a special election in 1978. Betty filed, ran, and won, serving in the Missouri House of Representatives for 10 years. Then she became the first woman to run for Governor in the state of Missouri against Republican John Ashcroft. No one else in Democratic politics was willing to take on the well-financed incumbent Ashcroft, even though they detested his policies. Betty, never one to duck from a challenge, jumped into the race to prevent him from having a free ride. She was completely outspent but made it a lively race, even though she didn't have sufficient funds to get her message out in a campaign age where media spots could make or break a candidate. After that loss, Betty attempted to return to her House seat in 1990 and then in 1992 for the Missouri Senate. Both campaigns were unsuccessful.

> **" Everybody should have equal access to the law. "**
>
> WARREN HEARNES

Following his Auditor's race, Warren was asked to take over as Executive Director of Southeast Missouri Legal Services. This federally funded program assists four to five thousand poor people to access legal services such as divorce, child custody, and bankruptcy.

"I found it rewarding," Hearnes said. "These people do need help. Everybody should have equal access to justice. From Legal Services, they get the same quality lawyer that other people get."

During his 16 years with Legal Services, Warren changed it to a Judicare system, which gave better service to people.

In the late fall of 1989, Warren and Betty opened the Hearnes Museum on the main street of Charleston. Over their many years in politics, the Hearnes had amassed a gigantic collection of photographs, letters, citations, and political memorabilia. Warren's idea was to throw it all away. Realizing its value to Missouri history, Betty had a better idea. The Hearnes took over an empty drug store and placed the items on display. Many politicians flew in for the grand opening, which brought together a large group of Hearnes friends and supporters from over the years.

Today, the museum is open by appointment only. Many school groups come through the doors, and during the renowned Charleston Dogwood/Azalea Festival, literally thousands of people pore over its exhibits.

Betty and Warren remain active in Charleston. Betty became Chair of the Mississippi County Industrial Authority, and Warren and she worked tirelessly to help bring the new correctional center to the county.

In 1995, the couple was awarded the Missouri Citizens for the Arts Advocacy Award, which pleased them both very much.

Betty has directed music in the First Baptist Church in Charleston for 30 years.

All the Hearnes children now live in St. Louis. Lynn is an attorney. Leigh is married to an attorney and has two children. Julie B. is married to a dentist and has two children.

As for Warren, he is semi-retired from Legal Services, acting as a consultant. He still goes to his law office for a little bit almost every day. He sits in his old Governor's chair that state employees bought for him and sits behind the desk set that appears in his official Governor's photograph. The walls are filled with photographs and political memorabilia from 50 years of public service.

Today, Warren and Betty are both still called upon for advice and help in local matters and by Democratic politicians. As has been their credo for all their married life, they always accept those calls for advice and assistance because they still believe in doing whatever they can to help make life a little better for others.

CHAPTER TEN
Legacy

"The next generation will not have the slightest idea what you did for public school education, or mental health, or anything. Down here, they only spend two hours in school teaching about World War II. What do you think they spend on teaching about a governor?"

WARREN HEARNES

Photo on previous page –

Hearnes' strategy as a political leader was informed by staying in touch with Missourians of all ages.

Courtesy of Missouri State Archives

As was the custom in ancient civilizations, our society still honors remarkable leaders by erecting buildings in tribute to them that bear their name.   Warren Eastman Hearnes certainly received his share. The Hearnes Multipurpose Building in Columbia, Hearnes Hall in Joplin, Hearnes Psychiatric Center and Hearnes Children and Youth Center in Fulton, Hearnes Learning Resource Center in St. Joseph, Hearnes Building at the Missouri State Chest Hospital in Mt. Vernon, and Warren E. Hearnes Elementary School in Charleston all bear his name.

Hearnes signed the first Public Accommodation Law ... the state's first civil rights law.

The Hearnes Museum in Charleston is filled with photographs, correspondence, and memorabilia of a man that was not just in the center of the political world of his time in Missouri but a man who interacted with all the prominent national political figures of his day.

Although these structures bear witness to the esteem Missouri feels for Governor Hearnes and the importance of his leadership during that time in Missouri history, his legacy will live on through the dramatic improvements he made possible in the lives of millions of Missourians and will continue to make possible in the lives of millions of Missourians for generations to come.

At a time in our history when great turmoil and unrest were the order of the day due to an unpopular war, the rise of civil rights, and a national protest movement...when America's great leaders were struck down by assassinations in rapid succession—John Kennedy, Martin Luther King, and Bobby Kennedy...his steadfast hand, firm convictions and enormous vision kept Missouri on the road to progress.

Warren Hearnes brought an uncommon understanding of government to his responsibilities as Governor. His service in the Missouri General Assembly as both a member and a leader and four years in the executive branch as Secretary of State prepared him well to become the state's chief executive.

A public official with broader experience better understands the importance of separation of power within government. Many of the impasses that develop in governance occur when public officials do not understand or respect the proper role of the various branches of government in the development and execution of public policy.

Later Hearnes would serve in the judiciary, making him one of the most unique of all Missouri public officials—a man who served in all three branches of government during his public service career.

He also stands apart as a man of uncommon political courage. He not only had the fortitude to buck the Democratic Establishment system that customarily anointed the candidate that would run for Governor on behalf of the party. He defeated the party's handpicked candidate. Then after four years as Governor, when he was well aware of how insufficient existing revenues were to keep Missouri moving forward, he made the boldest of all political moves. Rather than sitting idly by to watch Missouri slip into mediocrity, Hearnes called for a major tax increase—an act most politicians would equate with political suicide.

Granted, this action cost Hearnes some of his great popularity and a number of friends. Nor was he willing to back down when the plan was rejected the first time. Because he knew it was the right thing to do. Thus, he continued to fight until more revenue was approved. At a critical juncture, he kept Missouri on the road to progress, rather than sliding backward.

Therefore, in seeking the legacy of Governor Warren Eastman Hearnes, the answer is not to be found in buildings and tributes. The legacy of Warren Hearnes is found in the way his leadership touched the lives of every Missourian, the way his achievements continue to touch the lives of every Missourian today, and the way his accomplishments will touch the lives of the generations of Missourians to follow.

Every person who receives a Missouri education is better prepared because Warren Hearnes saw to it that Missouri could attract excellent teachers by treating them as the professionals they are with professional salaries and professional benefits...that schools and colleges had the resources they needed to send the best students out into the world…that Missouri had the vocational schools and junior and community colleges to help Missourians be successful in the world of work.

Every individual in Missouri who has dealt with mental illness or has a family member with mental illness can have hope that those affected will find healing because Warren Hearnes fought for treatment and brought Missouri's mental health system out of the dark ages of shutting patients away in institutions.

Every Missourian enjoys the advantages of a healthy economy because of the new and expanded business climate Warren Hearnes created in Missouri. Every Missourian who is elderly, disabled, or in need of assistance has stronger support to lead a quality life because of the programs Warren Hearnes implemented.

All Missourians can take pride in their state and the economic boon of the millions of visitors who discover our state every year because Warren Hearnes made tourism big business. Every Missourian benefits from the arts because Warren and Betty Hearnes championed their importance. All Missourians receive better services from their government because of the reforms championed by Warren Hearnes. Thousands of Missourians and visitors from other states learn to appreciate the glory of Missouri's past because Warren and Betty Hearnes held fast to the vision of the Governor's Mansion as the Missouri showcase it should be.

The success of Warren Hearnes is reflected in the success and happiness of every Missourian…in the lives we lead…in the state we treasure. That is his gift…that is his legacy as Governor of the Great State of Missouri.

At Missouri Western State University, St. Joseph • From the Hearnes Personal Collection

Afterword

*"You may yet change the world
but only if you begin with a practical view of yourself
and the realities of the world around you."*

Photo on previous page –

Portrait of Warren Eastman Hearnes, 1998

Lueders Studio, Cape Girardeau, MO • From the Hearnes Personal Collection

W hen Warren E. Hearnes stepped down as the 46th Governor of Missouri, it ended a career in public life that spanned 22 years. He began in 1951 as a young law student and a freshman member of the General Assembly.

After ten years in the General Assembly, four as the Majority Floor Leader, then four years as Secretary of State, and finally the first man to serve two consecutive terms as Missouri Governor, Warren Hearnes was only forty-nine years old when he left office.

Few would disagree that Warren Hearnes proved to be one of the most effective politicians in Missouri history. He used that ability to pass 19 major pieces of legislation out of 20 proposed in his first session, a record that few Missouri governors, if any, can match.

Most important of all from a personal perspective, he left office with the same unwavering faith in the value of public service that he held when he began that first run for a Missouri House seat. In one way or another, he has continued to serve the citizens of Missouri his entire life.

" The good experiences have far outweighed the bad. "

WARREN HEARNES

To conclude this memoir of a remarkable career in public service by such an extraordinary man, it seems only fitting that the last words would be his. Therefore, this memoir ends with his final public utterance as Governor as he stood at the dais in the beautiful chamber of his very first love, the House of Representatives, to address the Missouri General Assembly:

"My eight years as Governor have been marked by numerous friendships here in the General Assembly, with state and local officials and with citizens throughout our great state. The good experiences have far outweighed the bad, and I offer my deep thanks to those with

whom I have served and my warmest wishes to those who now move forward with the heavy responsibilities of government.

❝ ...all I have wanted from life has been given to me by the people of Missouri... ❞

WARREN HEARNES

"I have often been asked what this office I now leave has meant to me, and what advice I can offer to those who follow in the years to come. For my part, I can only say that all I have wanted from life has been given to me by the people of Missouri in eight short but wonderful years.

"For my successors, I must advise that you cannot even dream of the ordeal to which you surely will be exposed. You will experience a sensitive shrinking from undeserved criticism and this you must learn to control. You must fight within yourself the continual contest between a normal desire for public approval and your personal sense of public duty. Frequently your motives will be impugned and you will be subjected to the sneers and sarcasms of ignorance and malice.

"To keep such incidents from affecting your thoughts and actions, and to retain your integrity, you must learn to bear the burdens unmoved and to walk steadily forward in the path of duty. You will be sustained only by the persistent thought that time may do you justice, and that if it does not, then even your personal hopes and aspirations and your own good name are of little consequence when weighed against the welfare of a people of whose destiny you are the constituted guardian and defender.

"Thank you and goodbye."

LAURA & PAUL ADAMS, 94 DESIGN
LISA DAVIS
KEN WINN
LAURA JOLLEY, Missouri State Archives
MARGOT McMILLEN
AL SULLIVAN
LYNN HEARNES
ROSALIE LITTLE
PAT PETERSON

PUBLICATIONS

A HISTORY OF MISSOURI: VOLUME 6 by Lawrence H. Larsen

IF WALLS COULD TALK: THE STORY OF MISSOURI'S FIRST FAMILIES by Jean Carnahan

CLIPPINGS FROM A WIDE RANGE OF MISSOURI NEWSPAPERS (attributed when possible)

ST. LOUIS POST-DISPATCH Cartoon by Thomas Engelhardt (page 176)

FLY LEAF PHOTOGRAPHS

FRONT – A young Warren Hearnes, with shovel in hand, officiates at the Schwitzer groundbreaking in Rolla, Missouri.

BACK – A mature Warren Hearnes, with shovel and hard hat, participates as a senior statesman in the Southeast Correctional Center groundbreaking in Charleston, Missouri. Courtesy of Missouri Department of Corrections Public Information Office

❝ *Thank you, from the bottom of my heart, to everyone who made this memoir possible.* ❞

BETTY COOPER HEARNES

DISESTABLISHMENTARIANIST

St. Louis Post-Dispatch Cartoon by Thomas A. Engelhardt